Server-Side Enterprise Development with Angular

Use Angular Universal to pre-render your web pages, improving SEO and application UX

Bram Borggreve

Server-Side Enterprise Development with Angular

Author: Bram Borggreve

Reviewer: Juri Strumpflohner

Managing Editor: Taabish Khan

Acquisitions Editor: Aditya Date

Production Editor: Nitesh Thakur

Editorial Board: David Barnes, Ewan Buckingham, Simon Cox, Manasa Kumar, Alex Mazonowicz, Douglas Paterson, Dominic Pereira, Shiny Poojary, Saman Siddiqui, Erol Staveley, Ankita Thakur, and Mohita Vyas.

First Published: November 2018

Production Reference: 1281118

Published by Packt Publishing Ltd.

Livery Place, 35 Livery Street

Birmingham B3 2PB, UK

ISBN 978-1-78980-626-7

Table of Contents

Server-Side Rendering   57

Preface

About

This section briefly introduces the author, what the book covers, the technical skills you'll need to get started, and the hardware and software requirements required to complete all of the included activities and exercises.

About the Book

With the help of *Server-Side Enterprise Development with Angular*, equip yourself with the skills required to create modern, progressive web applications that load quickly and efficiently. This fast-paced book is a great way to learn how to build an effective UX by using the new features of Angular 7 beta, without wasting efforts in searching for referrals.

To start off, you'll install Angular CLI and set up a working environment, followed by learning to distinguish between the container and presentational components. You'll explore advanced concepts such as making requests to a REST API from an Angular application, creating a web server using Node.js and Express, and adding dynamic metadata. You'll also understand how to implement and configure a service worker using Angular PWA and deploy the server-side rendered app to the cloud.

By the end of this book, you'll have developed skills to serve your users views that load instantly, while reaping all the SEO benefits of improved page indexing.

About the Author

Bram Borggreve is a software engineer from the Netherlands, who currently works as an instructor at egghead.io, and is the founder of Colmena Consultancy. With almost 20 years of experience in all fields of the software lifecycle, Bram has a complete overview of the high-value challenges that clients are keen to resolve.

Objectives

- Identify what makes an Angular application SEO-friendly
- Generate commands to create components and services
- Distinguish between the container and presentational components
- Implement server-side rendering using Angular Universal
- Create a web server using Node.js and Express
- Add dynamic metadata to your web application
- Deploy a server-side rendered app to the cloud
- Implement and configure a service worker using Angular PWA

Audience

Server-Side Enterprise Development with Angular is for you if you are an experienced front-end developer who wants to quickly work through examples that demonstrate all the key features of server-side development. You need some prior exposure to Angular to follow through this book.

Approach

This is a fast-paced, practical hands-on book aimed at experienced developers. As you progress you'll find helpful tips and tricks, and useful self-assessment material, exercises, and activities to help benchmark your progress and reinforce what you've learned.

Minimum Hardware Requirements

For the optimal student experience, we recommend the following hardware configuration:

- Processor: i3
- Memory: 2 GB RAM
- Hard disk: 10 GB
- An internet connection

Software Requirements

You'll also need the following software installed in advance:

- Operating System: Windows 10
- Node 8.9.0 or higher
- npm 5.5.1 or higher
- Git
- Internet Browser: Google Chrome (latest version)

Conventions

Code words in text, database table names, folder names, filenames, file extensions, pathnames, dummy URLs, user input, and Twitter handles are shown as follows: "Running the **ng new** command will do the following:"

A block of code is set as follows:

```
cd angular- social

ng serve
```

New terms and important words are shown in bold. Words that you see on the screen, for example, in menus or dialog boxes, appear in the text like this: "You should be greeted with a default page that says **Welcome to angular-social!**."

Installation

Throughout the book, we will be using Node and npm to run our development environment, which is based on the Angular CLI. Additionally, Git is needed in order to retrieve content from https://github.com/. Please make sure your machine meets the following requirements:

- Node 8.9.0 or higher

- npm 5.5.1 or higher

- Git

To verify the installed versions, run the **node -v** and **npm -v** commands in a terminal.

If you want to install or upgrade to the latest version, please visit https://nodejs.org/.

Versions

While this book is written for Angular 7, most of the content will work exactly the same with Angular 6. We will do our best to keep the content of this book up to date, and in order to support future versions of Angular, we might add an errata.

Code Editor

Angular is written in and makes use of TypeScript, which is a superset of JavaScript that adds types. As a developer, you will get the biggest benefit from TypeScript if you use an editor that has good support for it. There are TypeScript plugins for most editors, but there are two we want to highlight, one free and one commercial option.

Visual Studio Code is a free and open source editor by Microsoft, which is the company behind TypeScript. This alone should give you confidence that the TypeScript support is amazing, which it is. VS Code runs on all major platforms. It can be downloaded from https://code.visualstudio.com/download.

WebStorm IDE is a commercial IDE by JetBrains, a company renowned for its solid IDEs. WebStorm also has great built-in support for TypeScript. There is a free community edition available for those who want to try it out at https://www.jetbrains.com/webstorm/download/.

Development API

This book focuses on building an Angular application that functions as a public website. It will retrieve the content from a REST API to match real-life use cases as closely as possible.

The development API can be downloaded from GitHub at https://github.com/TrainingByPackt/Server-Side-Enterprise-Development-with-Angular/tree/master/api and installed on your local machine:

```
$ npm install
$ npm start
```

If all went well, you should be greeted with this message:

```
Web server listening at: http://localhost:3000
Browse your REST API at http://localhost:3000/explorer
```

Additional Resources

The code bundle for this book is also hosted on GitHub at: https://github.com/TrainingByPackt/Server-Side-Enterprise-Development-with-Angular. Select the **solution** folder to access the code for the main theory and exercises. Select the **solution-extra-activities** folder to access the code for the activities.

We also have other code bundles from our rich catalog of books and videos available at https://github.com/PacktPublishing/. Check them out!

Creating the Base Application

Learning Objectives

By the end of the chapter, you will be able to:

- Build a modular Angular app using Angular CLI
- Implement a reusable user interface module based on the Bootstrap framework
- Implement application logic using a clean separation of concerns
- Use services to retrieve data from a REST API
- Use resolvers to make sure that the data is loaded before navigating to the page

This chapter introduces us to Angular CLI and how to use it to create a new application. Here, we will create the various components and implement the logic for our app.

Introduction

Server-Side Rendering

When we talk about the server-side rendering of websites, we generally refer to an application or website that uses a programming language that runs on a server. On this server, web pages are created (rendered) and the output of that rendering (the HTML) is sent to the browser, where it can be displayed directly. Examples of this include PHP, Java, Python, .NET, and Ruby.

Strengths

The benefits of server-side rendering is that the generation happens on a server, making it ready to consume in the browser once it's downloaded. It works great with indexing by search engines and with sharing on social media. The content is ready to be consumed, and the client (in this case, the search engine) does not need to run any code to analyze the page.

Weaknesses

The downside of server-side rendering is that the pages often have only basic possibilities of interaction with the user, and when the content changes, or the user navigates to another page, they have to re-download the whole page. This results in more bandwidth and gives the user the feeling that the page is loading slower than it actually is.

Client-Side Rendering

When we talk about client-side rendering, we generally refer to an application or website that uses JavaScript running in the browser to display (render) the pages. There is often a single page that is downloaded, with a JavaScript file that builds up the actual page (hence the term **single-page application**).

Strengths

The benefit of client-side rendering is that the pages are highly interactive. Parts of the page can be reloaded or updated without having to refresh the whole browser. This uses less bandwidth and it generally gives the user the feeling that the website or application is very fast. The server can be mostly stateless as the page is not rendered there; it just serves the HTML, JavaScript, and stylesheets one time and is done. This takes load off the server, and this results in better scalability.

Weaknesses

Client-side rendered websites are difficult for a search engine to index, as they need to execute the JavaScript to display how the page looks. This is also the case when sharing links to the sites on social media, since these are generally static instead of dynamic.

Another weakness is that the initial download is bigger, and this can be an issue on, for instance, mobile devices with slow connections. Users will see a blank page until the whole application is downloaded, and maybe they will just use a small part of it.

In this chapter, we will create an Angular application that is used throughout this book.

The Angular application we will build is going to be a list of posts that you regularly see on a social networking site such as Twitter. From the list of posts, we can click a link that brings us to the post detail page. We will intentionally keep the application simple as this book is meant to focus on the technology rather than the functionality of the app. Although the app is simple, we will develop it using best practices for Angular development. It should be easy for any Angular developer to extend on the logic and structure that is shown in this application.

Installing Angular CLI

Angular CLI is the officially supported tool for creating and developing Angular applications. It's an open source project that is maintained by the Angular team and is the recommended way to develop Angular applications.

Angular CLI offers the following functionalities:

- Create a new application
- Run the application in development mode
- Generate code using the best practices from the Angular team
- Run unit tests and end-to-end tests.
- Create a production-ready build
- Easily install and add third-party software (using **ng add**, since version 6)

One of the main benefits of using Angular CLI is that you don't need to configure any build tools. It's all abstracted away and available through one handy command: **ng**.

Throughout this book, we will be using the **ng** command for creating the app, generating the code, running the application in development mode, and creating builds.

> **Note**
>
> For more information about Angular CLI, refer to the project page on GitHub at
> https://github.com/angular/angular-cli.

Exercise 1: Installing Angular CLI

In this exercise, we will use **npm** to globally install Angular CLI. This will give us access to the **ng** command, which we will use throughout this book:

1. Open your terminal.

2. Run the following command:

   ```
   npm install -g @angular/cli@latest
   ```

3. Once this command has finished running without any errors, we can make sure that the **ng** command works as expected by running the following command:

   ```
   ng --version
   ```

   Verify that the output is similar to the output shown here:

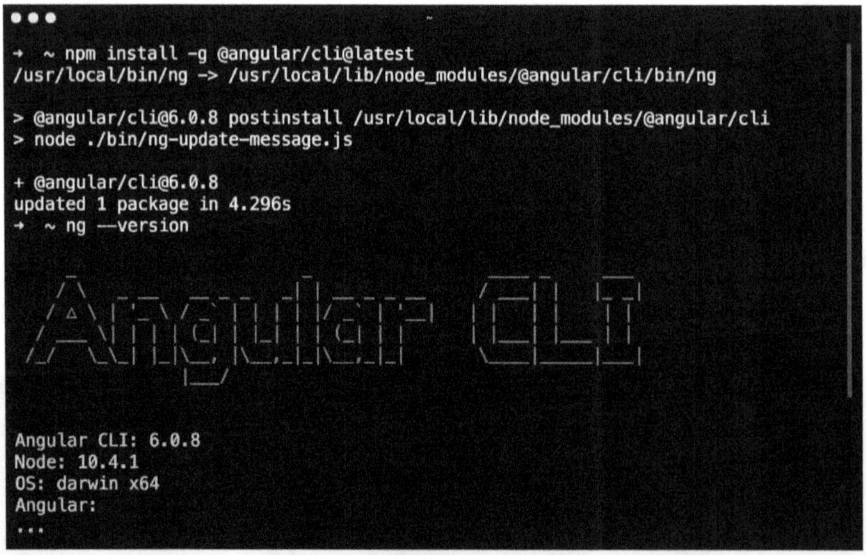

Figure 1.1: Installing Angular CLI

We now have Angular CLI installed and we are ready to get started!

Creating a New Application

Now that we have installed and configured Angular CLI, we will start by generating a new application.

Running the **ng new** command will do the following:

1. Create a folder called **angular-social**.

2. Create a new application inside this folder.

3. Add a routing module (because of the **--routing** flag).

4. Run **npm install** inside this folder to install the dependencies.

5. Run **git init** to initialize a new Git repository.

The following is the folder structure of an Angular CLI app:

- **src**: This folder contains the source files for the application.

- **src/app/**: This folder contains the application files.

- **src/assets/**: This folder contains the static assets we can use in the application (such as images).

- **src/environments/**: This folder contains the definition of the default environments of the application.

- **e2e**: This folder contains the end-to-end tests for the application.

Exercise 2: Creating a New Application

In this exercise, we will create a new application. Follow these steps to complete this exercise:

1. Open the terminal and navigate to the workspace directory where you want to work on the application:

   ```
   cd dev
   ```

2. Inside the workspace directory, invoke the **ng** command, as follows:

   ```
   ng new angular-social
   ```

3. Answer **Y** to the question about generating a routing module.

4. For the stylesheet format, we will select **CSS**.

   The application will be generated using these options in the **angular-social** directory, as shown in the following screenshot:

```
●●●                                        ng
→  dev ng new angular-social
? Would you like to generate a routing module? Yes
? Which stylesheet format would you like to use? (Use arrow keys)
❯ CSS
  SCSS    [ http://sass-lang.com   ]
  SASS    [ http://sass-lang.com   ]
  LESS    [ http://lesscss.org     ]
  Stylus  [ http://stylus-lang.com ]
```

Figure 1.2: Creating a new application

Exercise 3: Starting the Development Server

In this exercise, we will start the development server. Follow these steps to complete this exercise:

1. Open the terminal and enter the working directory:

   ```
   cd angular-social
   ```

2. Use **ng serve** to start the development server:

   ```
   cd angular-social
   ng serve
   ```

```
●●●                                        ng
→  angular-social git:(master) ng serve
** Angular Live Development Server is listening on localhost:4200, open your browser on http://localhost:4200/ **

Date: 2018-09-28T06:58:17.227Z
Hash: 00df32812930d3d5d5ee
Time: 6063ms
chunk {main} main.js, main.js.map (main) 13 kB [initial] [rendered]
chunk {polyfills} polyfills.js, polyfills.js.map (polyfills) 227 kB [initial] [rendered]
chunk {runtime} runtime.js, runtime.js.map (runtime) 6.22 kB [entry] [rendered]
chunk {styles} styles.js, styles.js.map (styles) 16.6 kB [initial] [rendered]
chunk {vendor} vendor.js, vendor.js.map (vendor) 3.65 MB [initial] [rendered]
ℹ ｢wdm｣: Compiled successfully.
```

Figure 1.3: Serving the application

Exercise 4: Browsing to the Application

In this exercise, we will navigate to the default page of our application. Follow these steps to complete this exercise:

1. Open your browser and navigate to **http://localhost:4200/**.

2. You should be greeted with a default page that says **Welcome to angular-social!**:

Figure 1.4: Browsing to the application

Configuring Global Styles

The default generated Angular application does not have any styling. Angular does not dictate anything in terms of style. This means that in your own projects you can use any CSS framework like Bootstrap, Angular Material, Foundation, Semantic UI, or one of the many others.

Alternatively, it's possible to create a custom style from scratch to get a unique look and feel. For this book, though, we will stick to Bootstrap 4 and Font Awesome, as they are widely used and provide a decent style with a minimal amount of code.

Font Awesome is a so-called **icon font**. You can include it in your page and then use it to show icons by applying some classes to an empty **<i class=""></i>** tag.

Linking to the Stylesheets in the Global styles.css File

As mentioned in the previous section, the application has a global stylesheet named `src/styles.css`.

In this stylesheet, we will use the `@import` command to link to Bootstrap and Font Awesome. This will instruct Angular to download those files and apply the style to the application globally.

> **Note**
>
> For a list of all available icons, you can refer to the Font Awesome icon list at https://fontawesome.com/v4.7.0/icons/. For an overview of all available Bootstrap styles, you can refer to the Bootstrap 4 documentation at https://getbootstrap.com/docs/4.1/getting-started/introduction/. To easily apply a different theme to the app, you can switch out Bootstrap with one of the BootSwatch themes at https://www.bootstrapcdn.com/bootswatch/.

Exercise 5: Installing Bootstrap and Font Awesome

In this exercise, we will add Bootstrap and Font Awesome to the global stylesheet. Follow these steps to complete this exercise:

1. Navigate to https://www.bootstrapcdn.com/.

2. From the main page, find the **Quick Start** block and copy the link that says **Complete CSS**.

3. Open the `src/styles.css` file in the editor.

4. Add the following line at the end of the file:

    ```
    @import url('');
    ```

5. Paste the link you copied in step 2 inside the quotes of the **url( )** function.

6. Navigate to the **Font Awesome** page on BootstrapCDN.

7. Copy the link to the CSS file.

8. Add the following line at the end of the file:

    ```
    @import url('');
    ```

9. Paste the link to Font Awesome CSS inside the quotes of the **url( )** function:

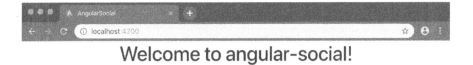

Figure 1.5: Import URLs

10. Refresh the app in the browser:

Figure 1.6: Applying a different font to the application

As you can see, the font of the application got updated to a sans serif font, as that's the Bootstrap default.

Exercise 6: Using Bootstrap CSS and Font Awesome

In this exercise, we will update the template of **AppComponent** to show that Font Awesome works. Follow these steps to complete this exercise:

1. Open the **src/app.component.html** file and replace its content with the following:

   ```
   <h1 class="text-center mt-5">
     <i class="fa fa-thumbs-up"></i>
   </h1>
   ```

2. When the app refreshes, you should see the thumbs up icon in the center of the page:

Figure 1.7: The thumbs up icon

Activity 1: Using a BootSwatch Theme

We can change the default Bootstrap theme with a different one. The **BootSwatch Themes** project (https://www.bootstrapcdn.com/bootswatch/) provides a lot of colorful themes that are a drop-in replacement for Bootstrap. This means that all of the Bootstrap CSS selectors will work – they just look different! In this activity, we will use a different theme for our app.

The steps are as follows:

1. Navigate to BootSwatch Themes (https://www.bootstrapcdn.com/bootswatch/) on BootstrapCDN.

2. Select one of the themes and copy the link to the CSS.

3. Update the link to Bootstrap CSS in **src/styles.css**.

4. Refresh the app in the browser and verify that the theme has been updated.

> **Note**
>
> The solution for this activity can be found on page 108.

Activity 2: Using Different Font Awesome Icons

Font Awesome comes with a large amount of icons that you can use once you've included the file. In this activity, we will use a different icon than the thumbs-up icon we have used already.

The steps are as follows:

1. Open the `src/app/app.component.html` file.

2. Navigate to the Font Awesome icon list at https://fontawesome.com/v4.7.0/icons/.

3. Replace the value of `fa-thumbs-up` with another icon. Note that you always need the `fa` class.

4. Refresh the app in the browser and verify that the browser now shows your new icon.

> **Note**
>
> The solution for this activity can be found on page 109.

Creating the UI for the Application

One of the great things about working with Angular is that it promotes building applications in a modular and componentized way. In Angular, `NgModule` (or simply `Module`) is a way to group an application into logical blocks of functionality. A `Module` is a TypeScript class with the `@NgModule` decorator. In the decorator, we define how Angular compiles and runs the code inside the module.

In this chapter, we are going to build a module that groups together the components we want to use in the application's global user interface. We will create a **LayoutComponent** that consists of a **HeaderComponent** and a **FooterComponent**, and in between those we will define the space where the actual application logic will be displayed:

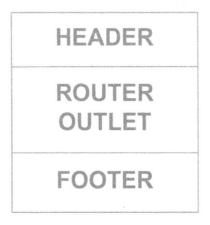

Figure 1.8: Structure of our module

Creating the UiModule

In this section, we will generate the **UiModule** using the **ng** command, import the **UiModule** in the **AppModule**, and add **Router Outlet** to the **AppComponent**.

Exercise 7: Creating the UiModule

Using the **ng generate** command, we can generate or scaffold out all sorts of code that can be used in an Angular application. In this exercise, we will use the **ng generate module** command to generate the **UiModule**. This command has one required parameter, which is the name. In this case, we use **ui**. Follow these steps to complete this exercise:

1. Open the terminal and navigate to the project directory.

2. Run the ng generate module command from inside the project directory.

   ```
   ng generate module ui
   CREATE src/app/ui/ui.module.ts (186 bytes)
   ```

   As you can see by the output of the preceding command, the **UiModule** is generated in the new folder called **src/app/ui**.

When we take a look at this file, we can see what an empty Angular module looks like:

```
import { NgModule } from '@angular/core';
import { CommonModule } from '@angular/common';

@NgModule({
  imports: [
    CommonModule
  ],
  declarations: []
})
export class UiModule { }
```

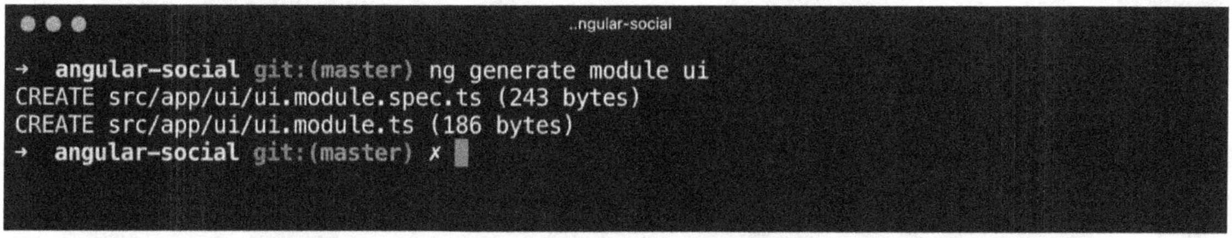

```
→  angular-social git:(master) ng generate module ui
CREATE src/app/ui/ui.module.spec.ts (243 bytes)
CREATE src/app/ui/ui.module.ts (186 bytes)
→  angular-social git:(master) ✗ █
```

Figure 1.9: Generating the UI module

Exercise 8: Importing the UiModule

Now that the **UiModule** has been created, we need to import it from the **AppModule**. This way, we can use the code inside the **UiModule** from other code that lives inside the **AppModule**. Follow these steps to complete this exercise:

1. In the editor, open the **src/app/app.module.ts** file.

2. Add the **import** statement at the top of the file:

    ```
    import { UiModule } from './ui/ui.module';
    ```

3. Add a reference to **UiModule** in the **imports** array inside the **NgModule** decorator:

    ```
    @NgModule({
      ...
      imports: [
        // other imports
        UiModule
      ],
      ...
    })
    ```

The **UiModule** has now been created and imported in the **AppModule**, which makes it ready to use:

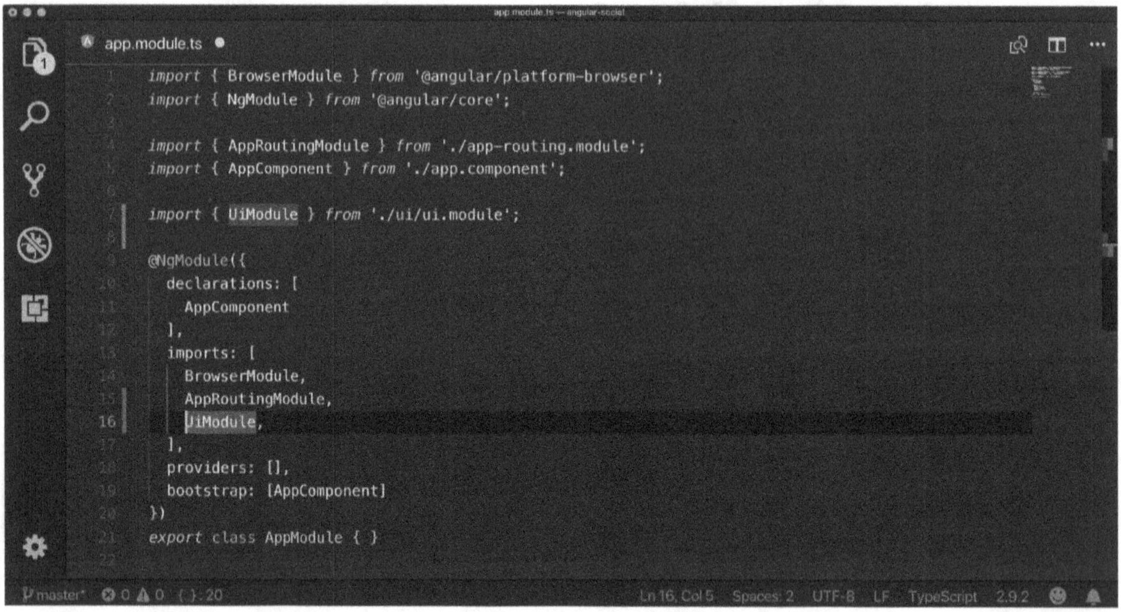

```
import { BrowserModule } from '@angular/platform-browser';
import { NgModule } from '@angular/core';

import { AppRoutingModule } from './app-routing.module';
import { AppComponent } from './app.component';

import { UiModule } from './ui/ui.module';

@NgModule({
  declarations: [
    AppComponent
  ],
  imports: [
    BrowserModule,
    AppRoutingModule,
    UiModule,
  ],
  providers: [],
  bootstrap: [AppComponent]
})
export class AppModule { }
```

Figure 1.10: Importing the UI module

Let's go ahead and create the first component inside the **UiModule** to make it display in the app!

Exercise 9: Updating the AppComponent Template

When building an Angular app, you generally lean on Angular's router to tie all of the modules and components together. We will build all the application logic in modules and use the **AppComponent** to display the current route.

For this to work, we need to update the **AppComponent** template and define the **router-outlet** component. Follow these steps to complete this exercise:

1. In the editor, open the **src/app/app.component.html** file.

2. Remove all of its content and add the following tag:

    ```
    <router-outlet></router-outlet>
    ```

Figure 1.11: Updating the template

After refreshing the app, we should see a blank page. This is because we don't have any routes set up, and thus there is no way that the Angular app knows what to display.

Let's move to the next topic so that we can create the basic layout.

Creating the Layout Component

In this section, you will use **ng generate** to create the **LayoutComponent** inside the **UiModule**, add the **LayoutComponent** to the **AppRoutingModule** so that it gets displayed, and implement the template of the **LayoutComponent**.

The **LayoutComponent** is the main template of the application. The function of this component is to glue together the **HeaderComponent** and the **FooterComponent** and show the actual application pages in between those two.

Exercise 10: Generating the LayoutComponent

In this exercise, we will use the **ng generate** command to create the **LayoutComponent**. Follow these steps to complete this exercise:

1. Open the terminal in the project directory.

2. Run the following command from inside the project directory:

    ```
    ng generate component ui/components/layout
    CREATE src/app/ui/components/layout/layout.component.css (0 bytes)
    CREATE src/app/ui/components/layout/layout.component.html (25 bytes)
    CREATE src/app/ui/components/layout/layout.component.spec.ts (628 bytes)
    CREATE src/app/ui/components/layout/layout.component.ts (269 bytes)
    UPDATE src/app/ui/ui.module.ts (273 bytes)
    ```

    We can see that the component was created in the new **src/app/ui/components** directory:

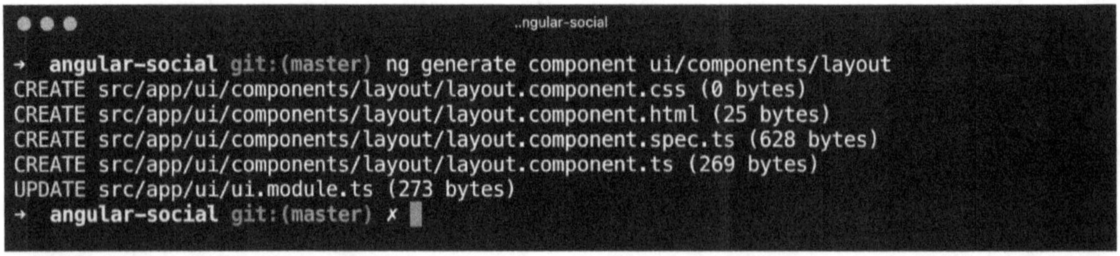

Figure 1.12: Generating the layout component

The last line of the output shows us that the **UiModule** got updated.

When we open the **UiModule** in the editor, we can see that it added an import for the **LayoutModule** and added it to the **declarations** array in the **NgModule** decorator.

Using declarations, we *declare* the existence of components in a module so that Angular knows that they exist and can be used:

```typescript
import { NgModule } from '@angular/core';
import { CommonModule } from '@angular/common';
import { LayoutComponent } from './components/layout/layout.component';

@NgModule({
  imports: [
    CommonModule
  ],
  declarations: [LayoutComponent]
})
export class UiModule { }
```

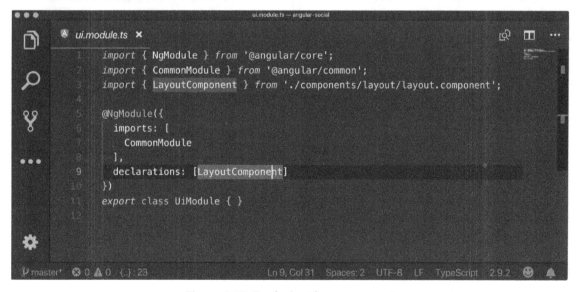

Figure 1.13: Declaring the component

Exercise 11: Adding the LayoutComponent to the AppRoutingModule

As described in the introduction of this section, we will use the **LayoutComponent** as the base for the whole application. It will display the header, footer, and a router outlet to show the actual application screens. We will leverage Angular's built-in routing mechanism to do this. We will add a new route to the routing array and reference the **LayoutComponent** in this route's component.

Follow these steps to complete this exercise:

1. Open the **src/app/app-routing.module.ts** file.

2. Add an **import** statement to the list of imports at the top of the file:

    ```
    import { LayoutComponent } from './ui/components/layout/layout.component';
    ```

3. Inside the empty array that is assigned to the **routes** property, we will add a new object literal.

4. Add the **path** property and set its value to an empty string, **''**.

5. Add the **component** property and set its value to reference the **LayoutComponent** that we just imported.

    The line of code that we must add to the **routes** array is as follows:

    ```
    {
      path: '',
      component: LayoutComponent,
      children: [] ,
    }
    ```

    For reference, the complete file should look like this:

    ```
    import { NgModule } from '@angular/core';
    import { Routes, RouterModule } from '@angular/router';
    import { LayoutComponent } from './ui/components/layout/layout.component';
    const routes: Routes = [
      {
        path: '',
        component: LayoutComponent,
        children: [],
    ```

```
    }
];
@NgModule({
  imports: [RouterModule.forRoot(routes)],
  exports: [RouterModule]
})
export class AppRoutingModule { }
```

```
app-routing.module.ts — angular-social

Ⓐ app-routing.module.ts  ●

     1    import { NgModule } from '@angular/core';
     2    import { Routes, RouterModule } from '@angular/router';
     3    import { LayoutComponent } from './ui/components/layout/layout.component';
     4
     5    const routes: Routes = [
     6      {
     7        path: '',
     8        component: LayoutComponent,
     9        children: [],
    10      }
    11    ];
    12
    13    @NgModule({
    14      imports: [RouterModule.forRoot(routes)],
    15      exports: [RouterModule]
    16    })
    17    export class AppRoutingModule { }
    18

master   ✕ 0  ⚠ 0  {.}: 23              Ln 12, Col 1    Spaces: 2   UTF-8   LF   TypeScript   2.9.2
```

Figure 1.14: Adding the LayoutComponent to the AppRoutingModule

When the application refreshes, we should see the text **layout works!**:

```
●●●     Ⓐ AngularSocial          ×    +

← → C    ⓘ localhost:4200                                      ☆  😊  ⋮

layout works!
```

Figure 1.15: Layout component

Exercise 12: Implementing the LayoutComponent Template

In this exercise, we'll get rid of this default text and start implementing the template. Follow these steps to complete this exercise:

1. Open the **src/app/ui/layout/layout.component.html** file.

2. Replace the contents of the file with the following code:

```
<h1>header placeholder</h1>
<div class="container my-5">
  <router-outlet></router-outlet>
</div>
<h1>footer placeholder</h1>
```

When we save the file, we will see that the browser outputs a blank page.

Looking in the **Console** tab from Chrome Developer Tools, we can see that we have an error stating **Template parse errors: 'router-outlet' is not a known element:**.

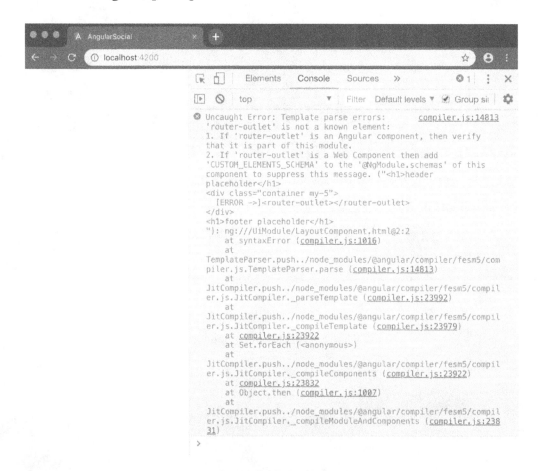

Figure 1.16: The router-outlet error

To make the **router-outlet** available to be used in the **LayoutComponent**, we need to import the **RouterModule** in **UiModule**.

3. Open **src/app/ui/ui.module.ts**.

4. Add an **import** statement to the list of imports at the top of the file:

   ```
   import { RouterModule } from '@angular/router';
   ```

5. Add a reference to the **RouterModule** inside the **imports** array in the **NgModule** decorator.

When we now save the file, we should see the placeholders for the header and footer, with some whitespace in-between and the router error gone from the console:

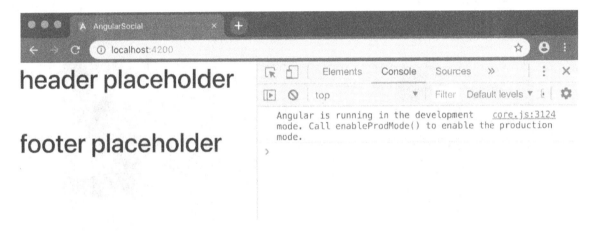

Figure 1.17: The header and footer placeholders

Now that that's done, let's add some content to the placeholders.

Creating the Header and Footer

In this section, you will download a logo to use in the application header, implement the header with a dynamic title and navigation items, and implement the footer with dynamic text.

Downloading the Angular Logo

We will now download the Angular logo and place it in the assets folder:

1. Download the **https://angular.io/assets/images/logos/angular/angular.svg** file.

2. Save the file as **src/assets/logo.svg** in the project directory.

Exercise 13: Adding the Header to the LayoutComponent

In this exercise, we will add the header to **LayoutComponent**. We will define three class properties: a string for the application logo, a title, and an array of objects that represent the navigation items we want to display in the header.

In the template, we will create a Bootstrap **navbar** consisting of a **nav** element with some styles, a link with the logo, the title, and the navigation items. Follow these steps to complete this exercise:

1. In the editor, open the **src/app/ui/components/layout/layout.component.ts** file.

2. Inside the component class, we will add some new properties:

    ```
    public logo = 'assets/logo.svg';
    public title = 'Angular Social';
    public items = [{ label: 'Posts', url: '/posts'}];
    ```

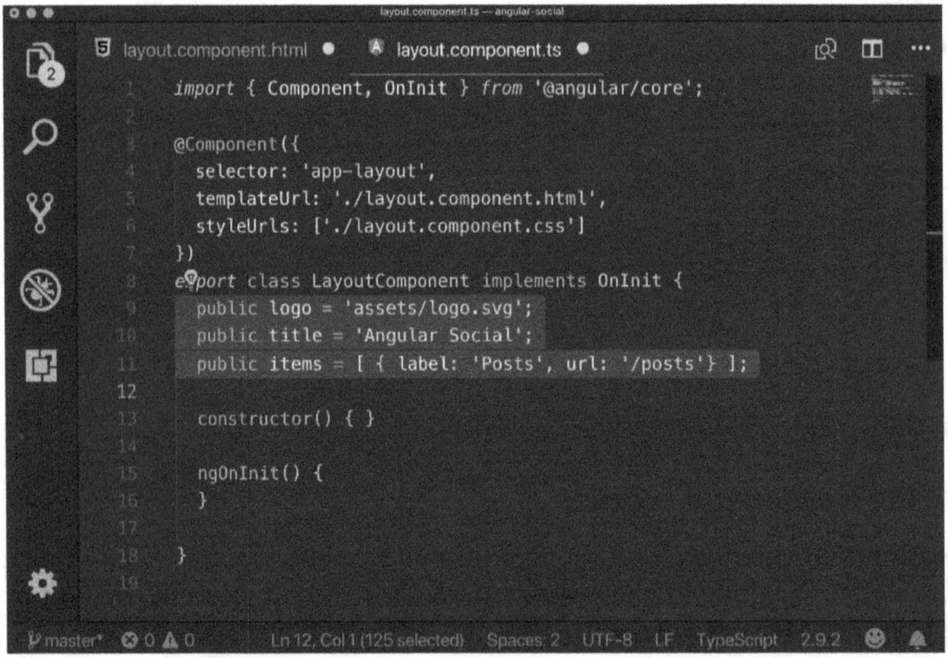

Figure 1.18: Adding the header

3. In the editor, open the **src/app/ui/components/layout/layout.component.html** file.

4. Replace the contents of the header placeholder with the following markup:

```html
<nav class="navbar navbar-expand navbar-dark bg-dark">
  <a class="navbar-brand" routerLink="/">
    <img [src]="logo" width="30" height="30" alt="">
    {{title}}
  </a>
  <div class="collapse navbar-collapse">
    <ul class="navbar-nav">
      <li class="nav-item" *ngFor="let item of items"
routerLinkActive="active">
        <a class="nav-link" [routerLink]="item.url">
          {{item.label}}
        </a>
      </li>
    </ul>
  </div>
</nav>
```

```html
 1    <nav class="navbar navbar-expand navbar-dark bg-dark">
 2     <a class="navbar-brand" routerLink="/">
 3      <img [src]="logo" width="30" height="30" alt="">
 4       {{title}}
 5     </a>
 6     <div class="collapse navbar-collapse">
 7       <ul class="navbar-nav">
 8        <li class="nav-item" *ngFor="let item of items" routerLinkActive="active">
 9         <a class="nav-link" [routerLink]="item.url">
10           {{item.label}}
11         </a>
12        </li>
13       </ul>
14     </div>
15    </nav>
16    <div class="container my-5">
17     <router-outlet></router-outlet>
18    </div>
19    <h1>footer placeholder</h1>
20
```

Figure 1.19: The header markup

When we save this file and check in the browser, we will finally see the first part of the application being displayed:

footer placeholder

Figure 1.20: The header

Exercise 14: Adding the Footer to the LayoutComponent

In this exercise, we will add the footer to the **LayoutComponent**.

We will define two class properties, a string property for the name of the developer and the year.

In the template, we will create another Bootstrap **navbar** consisting of a **nav** element with some styles and the copyright message that uses both string properties we defined in our component class. Follow these steps to complete this exercise:

1. In the editor, open the **src/app/ui/components/layout/layout.component.ts** file.

2. Inside the component class, we will add the following property. Don't forget to update the two placeholders with the right data:

```
public developer = 'YOUR_NAME_PLACEHOLDER';
public year = 'YEAR_PLACEHOLDER';
```

```
layout.component.ts — angular-social

□ layout.component.html        Ⓐ layout.component.ts  ●

1   import { Component, OnInit } from '@angular/core';
2
3   @Component({
4     selector: 'app-layout',
5     templateUrl: './layout.component.html',
6     styleUrls: ['./layout.component.css']
7   })
8   export class LayoutComponent implements OnInit {
9     public logo = 'assets/logo.svg';
10     public title = 'Angular Social';
11     public items = [ { label: 'Posts', url: '/posts'} ];
12     💡
13     public developer = 'Bram Borggreve';
14     public year = '2018';
15
16     constructor() { }
17
18     ngOnInit() {
19     }
20
21   }
22

⑂ master*  ✕ 0 ⚠ 0  {.} 25                    Ln 15, Col 1 (63 selected)   Spaces: 2   UTF-8   LF   TypeScript   2.9.2   😊   🔔
```

Figure 1.21: Adding the footer

3. In the editor, open the **src/app/ui/components/layout/layout.component.html** file.

4. Replace the footer placeholder with the following markup:

```html
<nav class="navbar fixed-bottom navbar-expand navbar-dark bg-dark">
  <div class="navbar-text m-auto">
  {{developer}} <i class="fa fa-copyright"></i> {{year}}
  </div>
</nav>
```

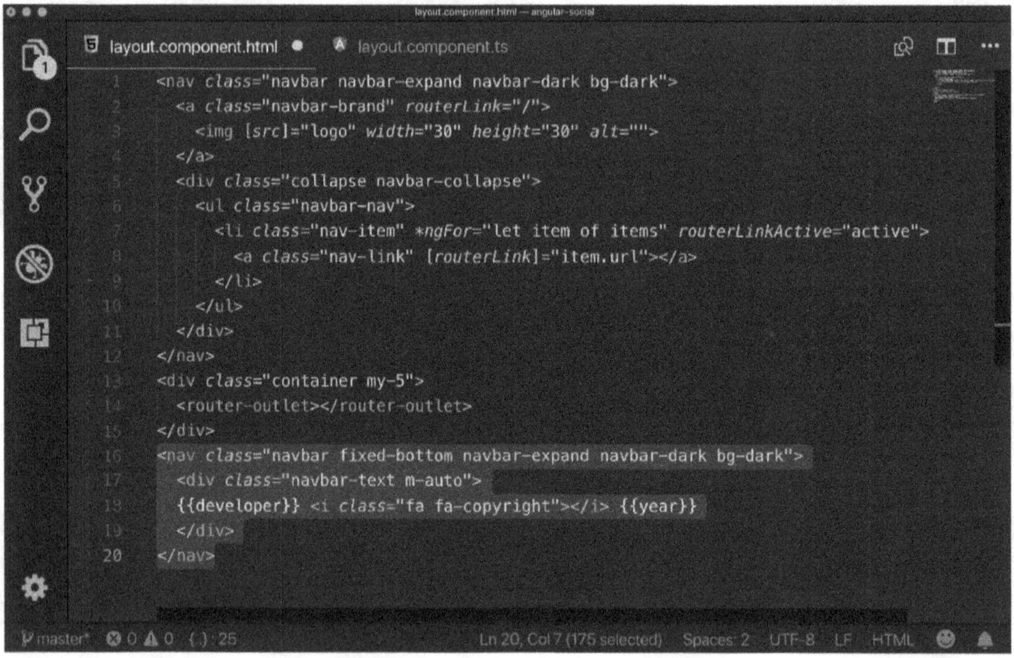

Figure 1.22: The footer markup

When we save this file and check it in the browser, we will see that both the header and footer are being displayed:

Figure 1.23: The header and footer

We are done with the layout. Let's start building the actual application logic.

We can refactor the **UiModule** by creating separate components for the header and the footer. The following activities should be completed using the knowledge that you have learned in this section.

Activity 3: Moving the Header to a Separate Component

In this activity, you will create a **HeaderComponent** in **src/app/ui/components/**. Reference the **HeaderComponent** in the **LayoutComponent** so that it says **header works!**.

After you have done this, you can copy the header markup and class properties from the **LayoutComponent** to the **HeaderComponent**.

The steps are as follows:

1. Create a component called **HeaderComponent**.

2. Use the selector to reference the **HeaderComponent** from the **LayoutComponent**.

3. Move the header markup from **layout.component.html** to **header.component.html**.

4. Move the header class properties from **layout.component.ts** to **header.component.ts**.

> **Note**
>
> The solution for this activity can be found on page 110.

Activity 4: Moving the Footer to a Separate Component

In this activity, we will create a **FooterComponent**, similar to and based on the instructions from the previous activity.

The steps are as follows:

1. Create a component called **FooterComponent**.

2. Use the selector to reference the **FooterComponent** from the **LayoutComponent**.

3. Move the footer markup from **layout.component.html** to **footer.component.html**.

4. Move the footer class properties from **layout.component.ts** to **footer.component.ts**.

> **Note**
>
> The solution for this activity can be found on page 111.

Creating the App Logic

In this topic, we will build the actual logic of the application.

We will create the **PostModule**, which contains all of the code related to displaying the posts that come from our API. Inside this module, we will add various components: a service and two resolvers. The components are used to display the data in the browser. We will go over their use in the next section. The service will be used to retrieve the data from the API. Lastly, we will add resolvers to the app that make sure the data from the service is available at the moment we navigate from one route to another.

Types of Components

In this topic, we will take a look at how we can differentiate our components by making a distinction between the **container** and **presentational** components. Sometimes, they are also called *smart* and *dumb* components when referred to how much *knowledge* of the world outside of the components each of them has.

The main difference we can make is this:

- A presentational component is responsible for how things look
- A container component is responsible for how things work

We will dive into more details of why this distinction is important when we create them, but we can give away a few things already.

Presentational components do the following:

- Get their data *passed in* using the **@Input()** decorator.
- Any operations are *passed up* using the **@Output()** decorator.
- Handle the markup and the styling of the application.
- Mostly just contain other presentational components.
- They have no knowledge (or dependencies) of any routes or services from the app.

Container components do the following:

- Retrieve their data from a service or a resolver
- Handle the operations that they receive from the presentational components
- Have very little markup and styling
- Will often contain both presentational and container components

The Folder Structure

To make this distinction clear in our project, we will use different folders for both types of components:

- The **src/<module>/components** folder is where the presentational components live.
- The **src/<module>/containers** folder is where the containers components live.

Creating the Module

In this section, we will create a module called **Post**. The **Post** module is responsible for retrieving the posts from an API and showing them in the app.

In this chapter, you will generate the **PostModule** using the **ng** command and lazy load the **PostModule** in the **AppRoutingModule**.

> **Tip**
>
> You can use shortcuts for most **ng** commands, for example, **ng generate module** can be shortened to **ng g m**.

Exercise 15: Generating the PostModule

We will use the **ng generate module** command to generate the **PostModule**.

This command has one required parameter name, and we will call this module **post**. A second optional parameter, **--routing**, is passed to create a file to hold the routes for this module, that is, the **PostRoutingModule**. Follow these steps to complete this exercise:

1. Open your terminal and navigate to the project directory.
2. Run the following command from inside the project directory:

```
ng g m post --routing
CREATE src/app/post/post-routing.module.ts (247 bytes)
CREATE src/app/post/post.module.spec.ts (259 bytes)
CREATE src/app/post/post.module.ts (271 bytes)
```

As you can see by the output of the preceding command, the **PostModule** is generated in the new folder **src/app/posts**.

Exercise 16: Lazy Loading the PostModule

In contrast to how we load the **UiModule** by importing it into the **AppModule**, we will lazy load this module using the **AppRoutingModule**.

This is an optimization on how the application gets built, and it makes sure that the application has a smaller initial file to download by using a technology called **code splitting**. This basically bundles each lazy loaded module into its own file, and the browser is instructed to download this file when needed, but not before.

We will add two routes to the main application file. The first route is a route with a blank **path** property (the default route), and its function is to redirect to the **/posts** route.

The second route is the **/posts** route, and it lazy loads the **PostModule**. If the user navigates to the app, the first route that will be found is the blank redirect route. This will tell the router to navigate to **/posts**. The router finds the **/posts** route and navigates the user to that module. Follow these steps to complete this exercise:

1. In the editor, open the **src/app/app-routing.module.ts** file.

2. Locate the existing **route** object that is defined in the **routes** property.

3. Inside the **children** array, we will create two routes that look like this:

```
{
  path: '',
  redirectTo: '/posts',
  pathMatch: 'full',
},
{
  path: 'posts',
  loadChildren: './post/post.module#PostModule',
},
```

Make sure that the complete routes property looks like this:

```
const routes: Routes = [
{
  path: '',
  component: LayoutComponent,
  children: [
  {
    path: '',
    redirectTo: '/posts',
    pathMatch: 'full',
  },
```

```
  {
    path: 'posts',
    loadChildren: './post/post.module#PostModule',
  },
  ],
}
];
```

We'll now see how this works:

- First, we define that we want to have children to the main route. This makes sure that all of the children get rendered in the **<router-outlet>** that is defined in the **LayoutComponent** in the previous section.

- We define the first route to respond to all paths (that's what the empty string does), and we make it redirect to the **/posts** route.

- Lastly, we create a **posts** route and we tell it to load its children from the new module. The **loadChildren** property is what enables the lazy loading.

When we refresh the page, we can see that nothing changes in the app itself, but we can see that the URL has changed: it has redirected to **/posts**:

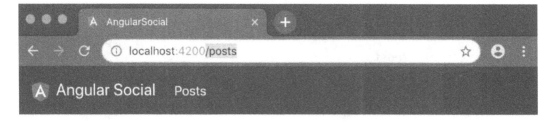

Figure 1.24: The redirected URL

Let's move on to the next topic, where we will create the container components so that we can start seeing data.

Creating the Container Components

In this section, you will use **ng generate** to create **PostListComponent** and **PostDetailComponent** inside the **PostModule**, add routes to both components, and create TypeScript models for our data objects.

Exercise 17: Generating the PostListComponent

In this exercise, we will be using the **ng generate** command to create our **PostListComponent**. This is the component that will eventually list an overview for all our posts. The application route to this component will be **/posts**. Follow these steps to complete this exercise:

1. Open your terminal and navigate to the project directory.

2. Run the following command from inside the project directory:

```
ng g c post/containers/post-list
CREATE src/app/post/containers/post-list/post-list.component.css (0 bytes)
CREATE src/app/post/containers/post-list/post-list.component.html (28
bytes)
CREATE src/app/post/containers/post-list/post-list.component.spec.ts (643
bytes)
CREATE src/app/post/containers/post-list/post-list.component.ts (280
bytes)
UPDATE src/app/post/post.module.ts (368 bytes)
```

3. Open the **src/app/post/post-routing.module.ts** file.

4. Import the **PostListComponent**:

```
import { PostListComponent } from './containers/post-list/post-list.
component';
```

5. Add the following route to the **routes** array:

```
{
  path: '',
  component: PostListComponent,
},
```

When we now refresh the page in the app, we should see the text **post-list works!** between our header and footer:

Figure 1.25: The PostListComponent

Exercise 18: Generating the PostDetailComponent

Very similar to the previous exercise, we will create the **PostDetailComponent**. This is the component that will be responsible for displaying an individual post.

The application route to this component will be **/posts/<id>**, where **<id>** is the identifier of the post we want it to display. Follow these steps to complete this exercise:

1. Open your terminal and navigate to the project directory.

2. Run the following command from inside the project directory:

    ```
    ng g c post/containers/post-detail
    CREATE src/app/post/containers/post-detail/post-detail.component.css (0
    bytes)
    CREATE src/app/post/containers/post-detail/post-detail.component.html (30
    bytes)
    CREATE src/app/post/containers/post-detail/post-detail.component.spec.ts
    (657 bytes)
    CREATE src/app/post/containers/post-detail/post-detail.component.ts (288
    bytes)
    UPDATE src/app/post/post.module.ts (475 bytes)
    ```

3. Open the **src/app/post/posts-routing.module.ts** file.

4. Import the **PostDetailComponent**:

   ```
   import { PostDetailComponent } from './containers/post-detail/post-detail.
   component';
   ```

5. Add the following route to the **routes** array:

   ```
   {
     path: ':id',
     component: PostDetailComponent,
   },
   ```

When the application refreshes and we navigate to **http://localhost:4200/posts/42**, we should see the text **post-detail works!**:

Figure 1.26: The PostDetailComponent

Exercise 19: Defining our Data Model Types

To get the most out of working with TypeScript, we will create some custom types to describe the data we get back from the API. We can use these types throughout the app, and they will help us during development by providing type information. This will, for example, prevent us from trying to access properties that do not exist, and can help with auto completion in the editor.

In this application, we will use a post and profile. Follow these steps to complete this exercise:

1. Open your terminal and navigate to the project directory.

2. Run the following command from inside the project directory:

    ```
    ng g class post/model/post
    CREATE src/app/post/model/post.ts
    ```

3. Open the **src/app/post/model/post.ts** file and add the following content:

    ```
    export class Post {
        id: string;
        profileId: string;
        profile: Profile;
        type: 'text' | 'image';
        text: string;
        date: Date;
    }
    ```

4. Run the following command from inside the project directory:

    ```
    ng g class post/model/profile
    CREATE src/app/post/model/profile.ts
    ```

5. Open the **src/app/post/model/profile.ts** file and add the following content:

    ```
    export class Profile {
        id: string;
        avatar: string;
        fullName: string;
        posts?: Post[];
    }
    ```

    We have now defined the two models. The last thing we need to do is import the **Profile** model from our **Post** model, and vice versa.

6. Add **import { Post } from './post';** to **profile.ts**.

7. Add **import { Profile } from './profile';** to **post.ts**:

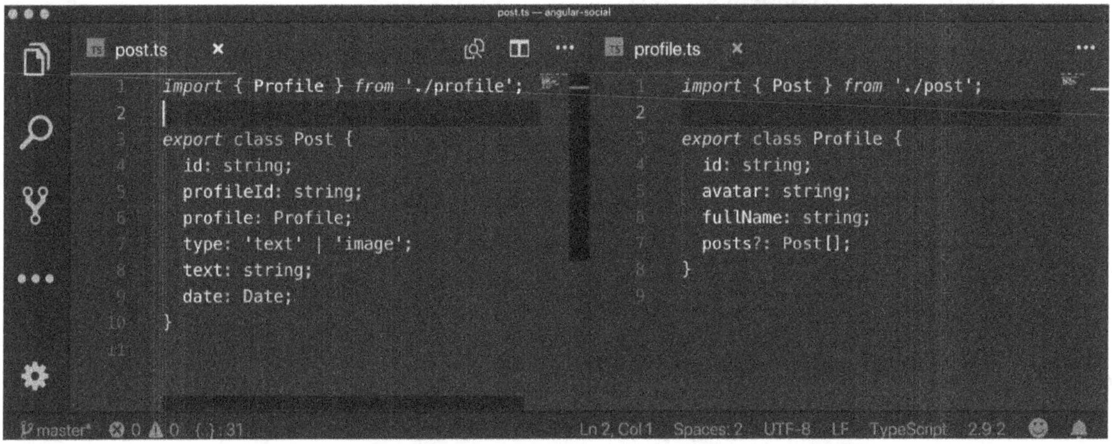

Figure 1.27: Importing our model types

Creating a Service for API Interaction

While you could make a request to an API from a component, the best practice in Angular is to use services for retrieving and sending data from and to the API. The benefits of doing this are that services can be reused throughout multiple components; this keeps the component to its responsibility of displaying an interface.

An additional benefit is that it makes your code easier to test when writing unit tests. You can mock the behavior of a service to make sure that the unit tests are not dependent on the API being online at the moment the tests are run.

Once we have created the service, we can inject it into a component and use it.

Exercise 20: Using the Environment to Store the API Endpoints

In this exercise, we will use the environment of Angular CLI to store the API URL. Using the environment, we can define a different URL for development and production environments.

By default, the application generated with Angular CLI comes with two pre-defined environments. These environments are defined in **angular-cli.json** in the default project.

Follow these steps to complete this exercise:

1. Open the `src/environments/environment.ts` file.

2. Inside the `environment` variable, add a key called **apiUrl** and assign the value to the `'http://localhost:3000/api'` string, which is the URL to the development API.

3. Open the `src/environments/environment.prod.ts` file.

4. Inside the `environment` variable, add a key called **apiUrl** and assign the value to the `'https://packt-angular-social-api.now.sh/api'` string, which is the URL to the production API.

Exercise 21: Generating and Implementing the PostService

In this exercise, we will use the **ng generate service** command to generate a service that will handle the interaction with the API. Follow these steps to complete this exercise:

1. Open your terminal and navigate to the project directory.

2. Run the following command from inside the project directory:

   ```
   ng g s post/services/post
   CREATE src/app/post/services/post.service.spec.ts (362 bytes)
   CREATE src/app/post/services/post.service.ts (133 bytes)
   ```

   The next step is to define two public methods in the **PostService** and make sure that these retrieve the data we need from the API. We will add two methods in the **PostService**.

   The first method is the **getPosts** method, which does not take any arguments and returns an **Observable** of all the posts from the API. The second method is the **getPost** method, which takes the ID of type string as an argument. It returns an **Observable** of the post with the ID that is passed in as an argument, and includes all the posts that are made by that profile.

3. Open the `src/app/post/services/post.service.ts` file.

4. Add an **import** statement to import the **HttpClient** from **@angular/common/http**, a reference to the environment where we have the API URL defined, and the **Post** model:

   ```
   import { HttpClient } from '@angular/common/http';
   import { environment } from '../../../environments/environment';
   import { Post } from '../model/post';
   ```

5. Define the **baseUrl** and **defaultParams** constants:

```
const baseUrl = `${environment.apiUrl}/posts/`;
const defaultParams = 'filter[include]=profile';
```

6. Update the constructor to inject the **HttpClient** and make it available under the private **http** variable:

```
constructor(private http: HttpClient) { }
```

7. Create a new method called **getPosts() {}** and add the following to it:

```
public getPosts(): Observable<Post[]> {
  const params = `?${defaultParams}&filter[where]
[type]=text&filter[limit]=20`;
  return this.http.get<Post[]>(baseUrl + params);
}
```

8. Create a new method called **getPost(id)** and add the following to it:

```
public getPost(id: string): Observable<Post> {
  const params = `?${defaultParams}`;
  return this.http.get<Post>(baseUrl + id + params);
}
```

Exercise 22: Using the PostService in the Container Components

In this exercise, we will reference the **PostService** in both the container components to fetch the data.

We will use the **OnInit** component lifecycle hook provided by Angular to call into the injected service and invoke the methods from that service. Note that we do the same thing for both the **PostListComponent** and the **PostDetailComponent**. Follow these steps to complete this exercise:

1. Open the **src/app/post/containers/post-list/post-list.component.ts** file.

2. Add an **import** statement for the new **PostService**:

```
import { PostService } from '../../services/post.service';
import { Post } from '../../model/post';
```

3. Add a **public** class property called **posts** of type **Post[]**:

```
public posts: Post[];
```

4. Update the constructor to inject the **PostService** and make it available under the **private service** variable:

```
constructor(private service: PostService) {}
```

5. Add the following to the **ngOnInit** method:

```
ngOnInit() {
  this.service.getPosts()
    .subscribe(
      res => this.posts = res,
      err => console.log('error', err),
    )
}
```

6. Open the **post-list.component.html** file and update the content to the following:

```
<pre> {{posts | json}} </pre>
```

Let's do the same for the **PostDetailComponent** now.

7. Open the **src/app/post/containers/post-detail/post-detail.component.ts** file.

8. Add an **import** statement for the new **PostService**:

```
import { ActivatedRoute } from '@angular/router';
import { Observable } from 'rxjs';
import { PostService } from '../../services/post.service';
import { Post } from '../../model/post';
```

9. Add a **public** class property **post** of type **Post**:

```
public post: Post;
```

10. Update the constructor to inject the **PostService** and **private route: ActivatedRoute** dependency:

```
constructor(private route: ActivatedRoute, private service: PostService)
{}
```

11. Set the contents of the **ngOnInit** method to the following:

```
this.service.getPost(this.route.snapshot.paramMap.get('id'))
  .subscribe(
    res => this.post = res,
    err => console.log('error' ,err)
  )
```

12. Open the **post-detail.component.html** file and update the content to the following:

```
<pre> {{post | json}} </pre>
```

Exercise 23: Importing the HttpClientModule to Enable the HttpClient

We are almost done creating the **PostService**, but there is still one thing we need to fix. When we refresh the application, we can see that we have an error message in the console:

```
ERROR Error: StaticInjectorError[HttpClient] :

StaticInjectorError[HttpClient] :

NullInjectorError: No provider for HttpClient!
```

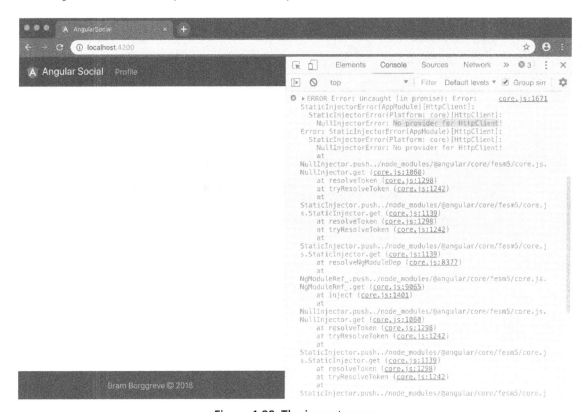

Figure 1.28: The import error

The reason that we get this error is because we have used the **HttpClient** in the service, but Angular does not know where this module comes from. To fix this, we need to import **HttpClientModule** in the **AppModule**. Follow these steps to complete this exercise:

1. Open the **src/app/app.module.ts** file.

2. Add an **import** statement to import the **HttpClientModule** from **@angular/common/http**:

   ```
   import { HttpClientModule } from '@angular/common/http';
   ```

3. Update the **imports** array in the **NgModule** decorator to import **HttpClientModule**:

   ```
   @NgModule({
   ...
     imports: [
       ...
       HttpClientModule,
       ...
     ],
   ...
   })
   ```

When we refresh the application, we should see a list of posts retrieved from the API:

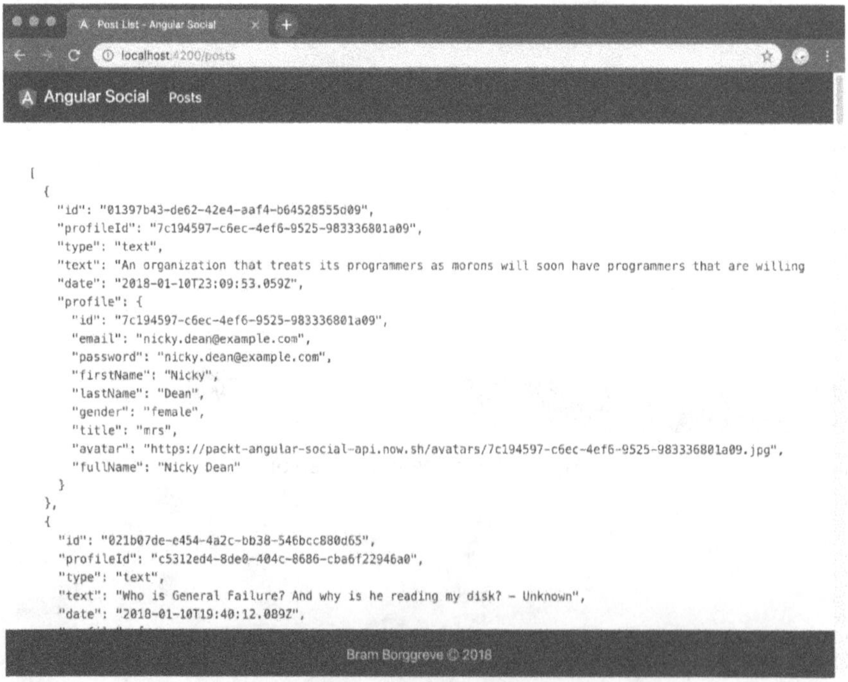

Figure 1.29: List of posts retrieved from the API

Let's continue and add some presentational components to give the posts some style.

Creating the Presentational Components

In this section, you will use **ng generate component** to create the **PostItemComponent** and **PostProfileComponent** inside the **PostModule**, implement the logic for these components, and use these components in our container components.

The **PostItemComponent** accepts a single post as its input and displays that post. For displaying the profile that belongs to the post, we use the **PostProfileComponent**. It takes the profile as input and uses the **ng-content** component to project the content on top.

Exercise 24: Generating the PostItemComponent

In this exercise, we will use the **ng generate** command to create our **PostItemComponent**. Follow these steps to complete this exercise:

1. Open your terminal in the project directory and run the following command:

    ```
    ng g c post/components/post-item
    CREATE src/app/post/components/post-item/post-item.component.css (0 bytes)
    CREATE src/app/post/components/post-item/post-item.component.html (28
    bytes)
    CREATE src/app/post/components/post-item/post-item.component.spec.ts (643
    bytes)
    CREATE src/app/post/components/post-item/post-item.component.ts (280
    bytes)
    UPDATE src/app/post/post.module.ts (574 bytes)
    ```

2. Open the **src/app/post/components/post-item/post-item.component.ts** file.

3. Import **Input** from **@angular/core** by adding it to the existing **import** statement and add the following:

    ```
    import { Post } from '../../model/post';
    ```

4. Add the following property in the component class:

    ```
    @Input() post: Post;
    ```

5. Update the template to the following:

```html
<div class="card">
  <div class="card-body" *ngIf="post">
    <app-post-profile [profile] ="post.profile">
      <div class="my-2">
        <a [routerLink] ="['/posts', post.id]" class="text-muted">
          {{ post.date | date: 'medium'}}
        </a>
      </div>
      <p>{{post.text}}</p>
    </app-post-profile>
  </div>
</div>
```

Exercise 25: Generating the PostProfileComponent

In this exercise, we will use the **ng generate** command to create our
PostProfileComponent.

This component will display the avatar and full name of the profile that created the
post, and it will use the **ng-content** component to show the markup that exists inside
the **<app-post-profile>** tags from the previous exercise. Follow these steps to complete
this exercise:

1. Open the terminal and run the following command from inside the project
    directory:

```
ng g c post/components/post-profile
CREATE src/app/post/components/post-profile/post-profile.component.css (0
bytes)
CREATE src/app/post/components/post-profile/post-profile.component.html (31
bytes)
CREATE src/app/post/components/post-profile/post-profile.component.spec.ts
(664 bytes)
CREATE src/app/post/components/post-profile/post-profile.component.ts (292
bytes)
UPDATE src/app/post/post.module.ts (685 bytes)
```

2. Open the **src/app/post/components/post-profile/post-profile.component.ts** file.

3. Import **Input** from **@angular/core** by adding it to the existing **import** statement and
    add the following:

```
import { Profile } from '../../model/profile';
```

4. Add the following property to the component class:

```
@Input() profile: Profile;
```

5. Update the template to the following:

```
<div class="media" *ngIf="profile">
  <img class="avatar mr-3 rounded" [attr.src]="profile.avatar" [attr.
alt]="profile.fullName">
    <div class="media-body">
      <h5>
        {{profile.fullName}}
      </h5>
      <ng-content></ng-content>
    </div>
</div>
```

6. Open **src/app/post/components/post-profile/post-profile.component.css** and add the following styles:

```
img.avatar {
  height: 80px;
  width: 80px;
}
```

Exercise 26: Using the PostItemComponent

In this exercise, we will use the **PostItemComponent**. Follow these steps to complete this exercise:

1. Open the **src/app/post/containers/post-list/post-list.component.html** file.

2. Update the template to the following:

```
<div class="row">
  <div class="col-md-8 offset-md-2 mb-3" *ngFor="let post of posts">
    <app-post-item [post]="post"></app-post-item>
  </div>
</div>
```

3. Open the **src/app/post/containers/post-detail/post-detail.component.html** file.

4. Update the template to the following:

```
<app-post-item [post]="post"></app-post-item>
```

When we now refresh the application in our browser, we can see that the content is styled and that the navigation still works as expected:

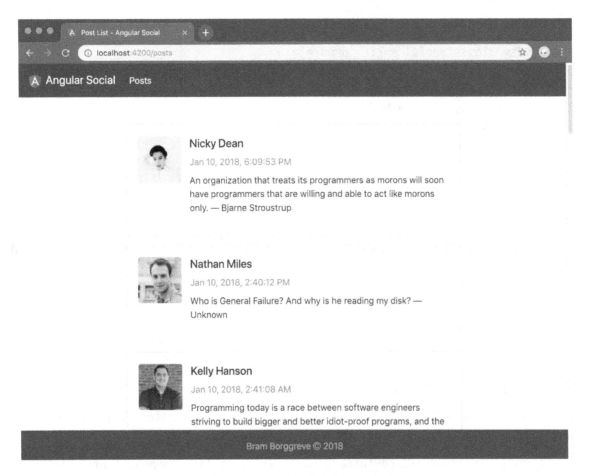

Figure 1.30: List of styled posts

We have successfully separated the concerns of retrieving the data and displaying it.

Resolving Data Using the Router

In this section, you will manually create two injectable classes that act as resolvers, configure the router to use these resolvers, and update the container components to use this resolved data.

A **resolver** is a class that we can use to fetch the data that we use in the component before the component is displayed. We call the resolvers in the routes where we need the data. In the implementation, the resolvers retrieve the data from the API and return it so that it can be displayed in the components.

> **Note**
>
> More information about resolvers can be found at https://angular.io/guide/router#resolve-pre-fetching-component-data.

Our application is quite neatly structured already, but there is one thing that we can optimize.

To see what the problem is, open Chrome Developer Tools and open the **Performance** tab. Hit the Cog icon and set **Network** to **Slow 3G**. If we now click around in the application, we will see that that the page navigation still works, but we are presented with empty pages.

The reason for this is that while the components are loaded correctly, they still need to retrieve the data after they are loaded. This is because the components call into the `PostService` from the `ngOnInit` method.

It would be better if the router could make sure that the component has all the necessary data loaded before entering the page. Fortunately, the Angular router provides a way to handle this by using resolvers. They will resolve the data before entering the route, and in the component, we can just take this resolved data and display it.

The resolvers that we create need the `@Injectable()` decorator to make sure that they are part of the dependency injection in Angular.

Exercise 27: Creating a Resolver for the getPosts Method

In this exercise, we will create a resolver that invokes the **getPosts()** method defined in the **PostService**. Follow these steps to complete this exercise:

1. Open a terminal and run the following command:

    ```
    ng g class post/resolvers/posts-resolver
    ```

2. Open the **src/app/post/resolvers/posts-resolver.ts** file.

3. Start the file by defining the necessary imports:

    ```
    import { Injectable } from '@angular/core';
    import { Resolve } from '@angular/router';
    import { Post } from '../model/post';
    import { PostService } from '../services/post.service';
    ```

4. Decorate the **PostsResolver** class with the **@Injectable** operator:

    ```
    @Injectable({ providedIn: 'root' })
    export class PostsResolver {}
    ```

5. Make the class implement **Resolve<Post[]>**:

    ```
    @Injectable({ providedIn: 'root' })
    export class PostsResolver implements Resolve<Post[]> {
    }
    ```

6. Inside the class, create a constructor and inject the **PostService**:

    ```
    constructor(private service: PostService) {}
    ```

7. Below the constructor, create a class method called **resolve** and make it return the **getPosts()** method from the **PostService**:

    ```
    resolve() {
      return this.service.getPosts();
    }
    ```

This is the resolver that will be used to retrieve all the posts, just like how we do this currently in the **PostListComponent**.

Exercise 28: Creating a Resolver for the getPost Method

In this exercise, we will create a resolver that invokes the **getPost()** method defined in the **PostService**. We will pass in the ID that we get from the **ActivatedRouteSnapshot**. Follow these steps to complete this exercise:

1. Open a terminal and run the following command:

    ```
    ng g class post/resolvers/post-resolver
    ```

2. Open the **src/app/post/resolvers/post-resolver.ts** file.

3. Start the file by defining the necessary imports:

    ```
    import { Injectable } from '@angular/core';
    import { ActivatedRouteSnapshot, Resolve } from '@angular/router';
    import { Post } from '../model/post';
    import { PostService } from '../services/post.service';
    ```

4. Decorate the **PostResolver** class with the **@Injectable** operator and pass in an object with the **providedIn** key set to **root**:

    ```
    @Injectable({ providedIn: 'root' })
    export class PostResolver {}
    ```

5. Make the class implement **Resolve<Post>**:

    ```
    @Injectable({ providedIn: 'root' })
    export class PostResolver implements Resolve<Post> {
    }
    ```

6. Inside the class, create a constructor and inject the **PostService**:

    ```
    constructor(private service: PostService) {}
    ```

7. Below the constructor, create a class method called **resolve**, and pass the **route: ActivatedRouteSnapshot** class into it:

    ```
    resolve(route: ActivatedRouteSnapshot) {
    }
    ```

8. Inside the **resolve** method, we return the **getPost()** method from the **PostService** while getting the **id** parameter from the **ActivatedRouteSnapshot**:

    ```
    resolve(route: ActivatedRouteSnapshot) {
      return this.service.getPost(route.paramMap.get('id'));
    }
    ```

This is the resolver that will be used to retrieve the posts that we have navigated to in the route.

Exercise 29: Adding the Resolvers to the PostRoutingModule

In this exercise, we will add the two new resolvers to the **PostsRoutingModule**. We will do this by importing the resolvers and then adding a **resolve** property to both of the routes. The **resolve** property takes an object where the key is how the data will be available in the router after it is resolved, and the value is a reference to the imported resolver. Follow these steps to complete this exercise:

1. Open the **src/app/post/post-routing.module.ts** file.

2. Import the two freshly created resolvers:

   ```
   import { PostsResolver } from './resolvers/posts-resolver';
   import { PostResolver } from './resolvers/post-resolver';
   ```

3. Update both the routes to add a **resolve** property and call into the resolvers:

   ```
   const routes: Routes = [
     {
       path: '',
       component: PostListComponent,
       resolve: {
         posts: PostsResolver,
       }
     },
     {
       path: ':id',
       component: PostDetailComponent,
       resolve: {
         post: PostResolver,
       }
     },
   ];
   ```

If we check the **Network** tab in Chrome Developer Tools, we can see that we make two requests to the same endpoint. This is because we retrieve the data twice: once in the resolver and once in the component. Let's update the container components and let them use the data resolved by the router.

Exercise 30: Using Resolved Data in the PostListComponent

In this exercise, we will update the **PostListComponent** to read the data that has been resolved by the router. We will subscribe to the data of the active route and we will map over that data twice. In the first **map** command, the **posts** value relates to the object key we used in the resolver object for this route. Follow these steps to complete this exercise:

1. Open the **src/app/post/containers/post-list/post-list.component.ts** file.

2. Import **ActivatedRoute** from **@angular/router**:

```
import { ActivatedRoute } from '@angular/router';
import { map } from 'rxjs/operators';
```

3. Remove the **PostService** import as we are no longer going to use it here.

4. Update the constructor to inject only **private route: ActivatedRoute**:

```
constructor(private route: ActivatedRoute) { }
```

5. Update the **ngOnInit()** method and replace the content with the following code:

```
ngOnInit() {
  this.route.data
    .pipe(
      map(data => data['posts']),
    )
    .subscribe(
      res => this.posts = res,
      err => console.log('error', err),
    );
}
```

Refresh the page and make sure that the data is still loaded.

Exercise 31: Using Resolved Data in the PostDetailComponent

In this exercise, we will update the **PostDetailComponent** to read the data that has been resolved by the router. We subscribe to the data of the active route and we will map over that data. In the **map** command, the **profile** value relates to the object key we used in the resolver object for this route. Follow these steps to complete this exercise:

1. Open the **src/app/post/containers/post-detail/post-detail.component.ts** file.

2. Add the following **import** statement:

    ```
    import {map} from 'rxjs/operators';
    ```

3. Remove the **PostService** import as we are no longer going to use it here.

4. Update the constructor to only inject **private route: ActivatedRoute**:

    ```
    constructor(private route: ActivatedRoute) { }
    ```

5. Update the **ngOnInit()** method and replace the content as follows:

    ```
    ngOnInit() {
      this.route.data
        .pipe(
          map(data => data['post'])
        )
        .subscribe(
          res => this.post = res,
          err => console.log('error', err),
        );
    }
    ```

Refresh the page and make sure that the data is still loaded.

In the following activities, we will introduce the **ProfileModule**, which is responsible for listing the profiles. The following activities should be performed using the knowledge that you have learned in this chapter.

Activity 5: Creating a ProfileModule

In this activity, you will create a **ProfileModule** in **src/app/profile**. Add a menu item in the **LayoutModule** to link to the new **ProfileModule**.

The steps are as follows:

1. Create a module called **ProfileModule**.

2. Define the **/profiles/** route to lazy load this new module in **app-routing.module.ts**.

3. Add a menu item to link to the **/profiles/** URL in the **header.component.ts** file created in *Activity 3*.

> **Note**
>
> The solution for this activity can be found on page 113.

Activity 6: Creating Container Components

In this activity, we will create the container components **ProfileListComponent** and **ProfileDetailsComponents**. The routes are similar to those in the **PostModule**.

The steps are as follows:

1. Add the **ProfileListComponent** and **ProfileDetailComponent** containers.

2. Add routes to the container components in **ProfileRoutingModule**.

> **Note**
>
> The solution for this activity can be found on page 114.

Activity 7: Creating Service and Resolvers

In this activity, we will create the service and resolvers called **ProfileService**, **ProfilesResolver**, and **ProfileResolver**. The functionality of those services and resolvers is identical to those in the **PostModule**.

The steps are as follows:

1. Add a **ProfileService** to retrieve the data.

2. Add a **ProfilesResolver** and **ProfileResolver** and use them in the **ProfileRoutingModule**.

> **Note**
>
> The solution for this activity can be found on page 115.

Activity 8: Creating Presentational Components

In this activity, we will create the presentational component to display the profile data.

The steps are as follows:

1. Use the resolved data in the container components.

2. Create the presentational components to display the profile data from the API.

> **Note**
>
> The solution for this activity can be found on page 117.

Summary

We started this chapter by installing Angular CLI and creating a new application. We configured styles using Bootstrap and Font Awesome. We then created the UI for our application, and we created the layout module and then the header and footer components. We finished this chapter by creating the application logic, including creating the container and presentational components, a service for API interaction, and routers.

Our basic application has been built, and even though there are enough things to add and optimize, it's well-structured and works using Angular's best practices. In the next chapter, we will add support for Server-Side Rendering by adding Angular Universal.

Server-Side Rendering

Learning Objectives

By the end of the chapter, you will be able to:

- Add support for server-side rendering using Angular Universal

- Build a server to host a server-side rendered app

- Add dynamic metadata to our pages

- Deploy the app to the cloud

This chapter shows us how to create a universal app, enable server-side rendering, and deploy our app to Docker.

Introduction

In this chapter, we will add server-side rendering to the application that we built in the previous chapter. We will use **ng generate** to add Angular Universal to our application, and add a few commands to **package.json** so that we can build the whole app in a single command.

We will implement a simple Node.js server based on NestJS. This server will compile and serve our application when requested so that the complete rendered app gets sent to the browser.

How does a Normal App Render?

First, let's take a look at how a normal Angular application without server-side rendering behaves.

When we start the server in development mode using **ng serve** and use the **View Source** option in our browser to check the source, we can see that the only thing that gets rendered is the output from file **src/index.html** file, with a few scripts appended at the bottom.

These scripts will be downloaded by the browser and after they have been downloaded and executed, the application will display:

```
1  <!doctype html>
2  <html lang="en">
3  <head>
4    <meta charset="utf-8">
5    <title>AngularSocial</title>
6    <base href="/">
7
8    <meta name="viewport" content="width=device-width, initial-scale=1">
9    <link rel="icon" type="image/x-icon" href="favicon.ico">
10 </head>
11 <body>
12   <app-root></app-root>
13 <script type="text/javascript" src="runtime.js"></script><script
   type="text/javascript" src="polyfills.js"></script><script
   type="text/javascript" src="styles.js"></script><script
   type="text/javascript" src="vendor.js"></script><script
   type="text/javascript" src="main.js"></script></body>
14 </html>
15
```

Figure 2.1: View source for our app

While this works in some situations, in others this can become problematic. If the user of your app is on a slow connection or slow device, it will take time to load and parse the scripts, and during that waiting time the user will see a blank page.

Another issue is that most search engines and social media sites will only read the initial payload of our website and will not download and execute our client-side JavaScript files.

In the following screenshot, we can see how a social media site will create a preview for the page. It cannot scrape the information from the page because it's not rendered:

Figure 2.2: Preview of our app

These are things that will be fixed in this chapter. After we have added server-side rendering, we will add support for dynamic metadata and page titles. This makes sure that any server-side rendered page has proper metadata, which will make these social previews rich in content and will make sure that search engines can index the pages properly.

There are online tools to verify how social media websites index your site.

In the following screenshot, you can see the **Card validator** from Twitter:

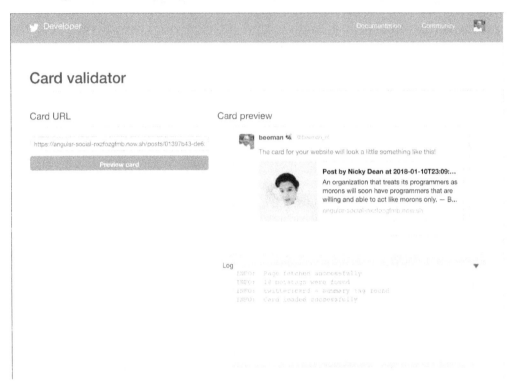

Figure 2.3: Twitter's Card Validator

Another site you can use is **Rich Preview** (https://richpreview.com/). Note that both sites require the app to be deployed to the internet before you can use them. You can't test your app on the local development environment.

One way to experience a slow connection on a normal Chrome browser is to open the **Developer tools**, go to the **Network** tab, and set the network speed from **Online** to **Slow 3G**.

When you load the page served by the server, you will get an idea of how long it takes for a slow connection to load the application:

Figure 2.4: The Network tab with network speed options

Generating the Universal Code

Since Angular CLI version 1.6, there is support for Angular Universal, and since version 6.x, it has been advanced even more. We can use the **ng generate** command to generate the majority of the code we need to add support for server-side rendering.

> **Note**
>
> **Schematics** is the name of the workflow tool that powers code generation in Angular CLI. You can write your own schematics to generate custom code using **ng generate**. If you would like to learn more about Schematics, you can refer to a blog post about it at https://blog.angular.io/schematics-an-introduction-dc1dfbc2a2b2.

Let's explore what happens when running the generator in more detail:

```
●  ●  ●                           ..ngular-social
→  angular-social git:(master) ng generate universal —clientProject angular-social
CREATE src/main.server.ts (220 bytes)
CREATE src/app/app.server.module.ts (318 bytes)
CREATE src/tsconfig.server.json (219 bytes)
UPDATE package.json (1361 bytes)
UPDATE angular.json (3896 bytes)
UPDATE src/main.ts (430 bytes)
UPDATE src/app/app.module.ts (576 bytes)
added 3 packages from 5 contributors and audited 24158 packages in 5.586s
found 14 vulnerabilities (9 low, 5 high)
  run `npm audit fix` to fix them, or `npm audit` for details
→  angular-social git:(master) ✗ ▏
```

Figure 2.5: Running the generator command

Running this generator will change a few things in the current app:

- It will add a new *architect* to the **angular-social** app in **angular.json**.

- It will add the **@angular/platform-server** dependency to **package.json**.

- It updates the **AppModule** and changes the **BrowserModule** import.

- It changes the way the *browser app* gets bootstrapped in **src/main.ts**.

Additionally, it creates some new files:

- It generates a new file called **src/app/app.server.module.ts** within the **AppServerModule**.

- The **src/main.server.ts** file exports the **AppServerModule**.

- A TypeScript config file for the *server app* is generated in **src/tsconfig.server.json**.

After the generator has added and updated the files, **npm install** gets executed to install the new dependencies.

Exercise 32: Generating the Universal Code

In this exercise, we will create the Universal code. We can use the **ng generate universal** command and pass in one required parameter, **clientProject**. The value of **clientProject** is your project name. In our case, it's **angular-social**. The project name is defined in **angular.json**. Follow these steps to complete this exercise:

1. Open the terminal in the project directory.

2. Run the generator to add the Universal app:

   ```
   ng generate universal --clientProject angular-social
   ```

3. Verify that the app still works as expected by running **ng serve** and visiting the app on **http://localhost:4200**.

Exercise 33: Building the Angular Universal App

In this exercise, we will build the Angular Universal app. Follow these steps to complete this exercise:

1. Open a terminal inside the project directory.

2. Run the following command to install the dependency:

   ```
   ng run angular-social:server:production
   ```

3. After the build is done, check the files in the **dist/angular-social-server** folder and make sure that it consists of the two files: **main.js** and **main.js.map**:

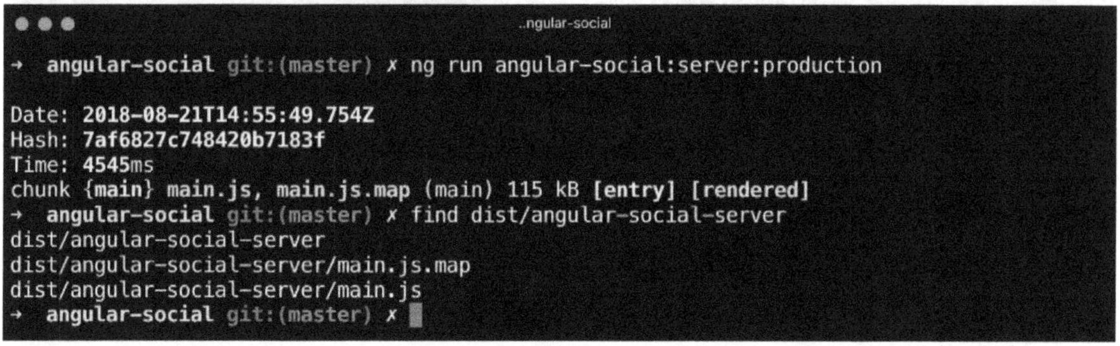

Figure 2.6: Building the Angular Universal app

Enabling Support for Lazy Loading

To get our server-side rendering working correctly, we need to make sure that we add the **ModuleMapLoaderModule**. This is a third-party module that is needed to make Angular Universal apps work with **lazy loading**.

In software development, we talk about lazy loading if we defer loading a certain object or piece of code to the point where we need it. In Angular specifically, this is done by defining certain *routes* to be loaded at the moment they are requested. The Angular build process will use *code splitting* to build lazy-loaded parts of the application in separate files. When the user then navigates to this part of the application, the browser will download that file and execute it.

The benefit of this approach is that the initial download size is smaller, and that a user does not have to download parts of the application that are not being used. This decreases the initial loading time of the application and potentially saves network bandwidth.

Exercise 34: Installing the ModuleMapLoaderModule

In this exercise, we will install and use the `ModuleMapLoaderModule`. Follow these steps to complete this exercise:

1. Open a terminal inside the project directory.

2. Run the following command to install the dependency:

   ```
   npm install --save @nguniversal/module-map-ngfactory-loader
   ```

```
● ● ●                              ..ngular-social
→  angular-social git:(master) npm install --save @nguniversal/module-map-ngfactory-loader
+ @nguniversal/module-map-ngfactory-loader@6.0.0
added 1 package and audited 24159 packages in 7.176s
found 14 vulnerabilities (9 low, 5 high)
  run `npm audit fix` to fix them, or `npm audit` for details
→  angular-social git:(master) x █
```

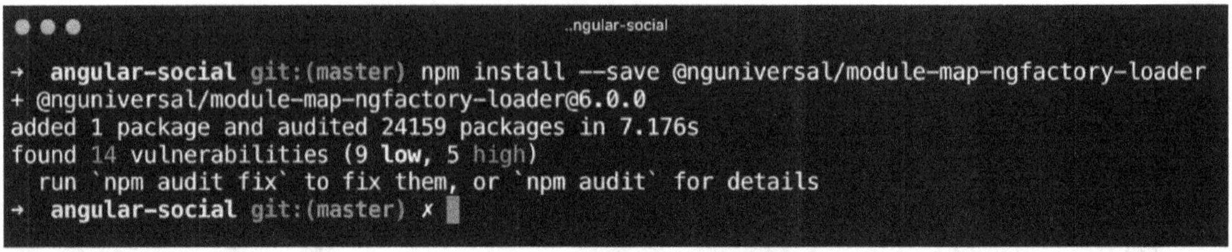

Figure 2.7: Installing the ModuleMapLoaderModule

3. Open the **src/app/app.server.module.ts** file in your editor.

4. Add the import at the top of the file:

   ```
   import { ModuleMapLoaderModule } from '@nguniversal/module-map-ngfactory-loader';
   ```

5. Add a reference to the imported module in the **imports** array:

```
imports: [
  ...
  ModuleMapLoaderModule,
],
```

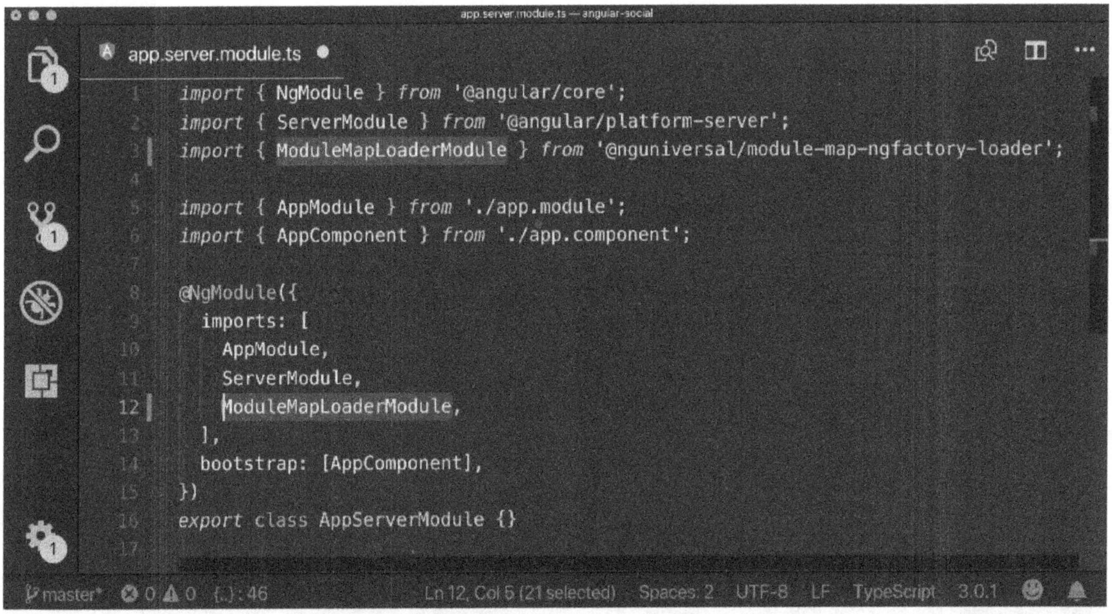

Figure 2.8: Using the ModuleMapLoaderModule

Exercise 35: Enabling initialNavigation in the AppRoutingModule

In this exercise, we will configure the **RouterModule** in **AppRoutingModule** to enable the **initialNavigation** option. This prevents the app from showing a white screen when the Angular browser application loads after the server-side rendered one. Follow these steps to complete this exercise:

1. Open the **src/app/app-routing.module.ts** file in the editor.

2. Add a second parameter to the **forRoot** method, an object with a key called **initialNavigation** set to **enabled**:

    ```
    {
        initialNavigation: 'enabled',
    }
    ```

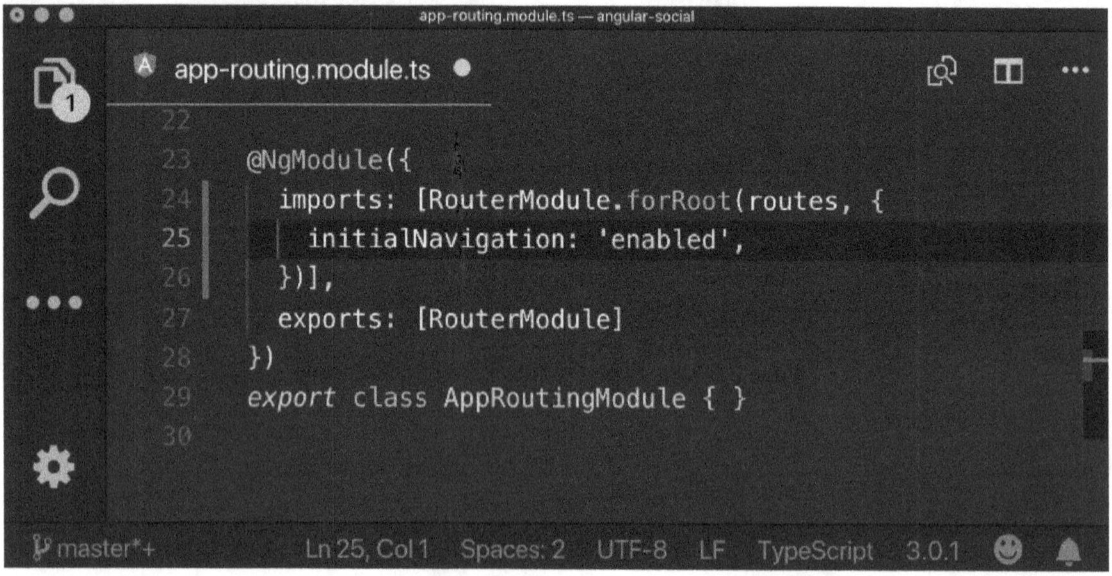

Figure 2.9: Enabling initialNavigation

Exercise 36: Adding the Build Scripts to package.json

In this exercise, we will add some *run scripts* to **package.json** so that we can build the browser app and the Universal app with one command. We will create two new scripts, **build:browser** and **build:server**, which build both parts. Once that's done, we'll update the existing **build** script so that it invokes both of the new scripts sequentially. Follow these steps to complete this exercise:

1. Open the **package.json** file in the editor.

2. Locate the **scripts** object and add the following scripts:

   ```
   "build:browser": "ng build angular-social --prod",
   "build:server": "ng run angular-social:server:production",
   ```

3. Replace the existing **build** command with the following:

   ```
   "build": "npm run build:browser && npm run build:server",
   ```

4. Verify that the **build** command works by running **npm run build**:

```
● ● ●                                 ..ngular-social

→  angular-social git:(master) x npm run build

> angular-social@0.0.0 build /Users/beeman/dev/angular-social
> npm run build:browser && npm run build:server


> angular-social@0.0.0 build:browser /Users/beeman/dev/angular-social
> ng build angular-social --prod


Date: 2018-08-21T15:00:14.904Z
Hash: e6105d01e88bb8213bbe
Time: 10969ms
chunk {0} 0.1416eb8625cf5bfb92a1.js () 5.45 kB  [rendered]
chunk {1} runtime.b00a4ba4283da90484cd.js (runtime) 1.84 kB [entry] [rendered]
chunk {2} styles.a46a8544723b3db246bc.css (styles) 178 bytes [initial] [rendered]
chunk {3} polyfills.9a5f6d04e0781d28c53e.js (polyfills) 59.6 kB [initial] [rendered]
chunk {4} main.ee1e9214a1d6122ebe7b.js (main) 295 kB [initial] [rendered]


> angular-social@0.0.0 build:server /Users/beeman/dev/angular-social
> ng run angular-social:server:production


Date: 2018-08-21T15:00:22.282Z
Hash: 7af6827c748420b7183f
Time: 4274ms
chunk {main} main.js, main.js.map (main) 115 kB [entry] [rendered]
→  angular-social git:(master) x ▌
```

Figure 2.10: Running the build command

Building the Server

Now that both of the applications can be built, we can move on to create a simple server to host the applications.

To do this, we will create a simple Node.js server built with **Nest**, a framework that uses Express.js and offers great support for running Angular Universal apps. Another great benefit of Nest is that the structure and terminology is inspired by Angular, so it's easy to understand how to extend the API.

We will build the server in the folder called **server** in the root, create a WebPack config to build the Nest server, and add a run script so that we can build the server using a single command.

> **Note:**
>
> The current implementation of Angular Universal depends on Node.js as it is implemented in JavaScript. It is possible to run Angular Universal apps using other servers like ASP.NET, though under the hood, the ASP.NET server will invoke a Node.js process to handle the Angular Universal part. An example repository of how to run Angular Universal can be found here: https://github.com/MarkPieszak/aspnetcore-angular2-universal.

Installing the Dependencies

First, we will install the dependencies we need to run Nest and also install the rendering engine that is used by Nest to load our Angular Universal app:

1. Open a terminal inside the project directory.

2. Run the following command to install the dependencies:

   ```
   npm install --save @nestjs/common @nestjs/core @nestjs/ng-universal @
   nguniversal/express-engine @nguniversal/common webpack-cli ts-loader
   ```

Exercise 37: Implementing the Nest Bootstrap file

In this exercise, we will implement our **server/main.ts** file. This file is responsible for bootstrapping the Nest **AppModule**, similar to how **src/main.ts** is responsible for bootstrapping the Angular **AppModule**. Follow these steps to complete this exercise:

1. Create the **server** folder in the root of the project.

2. In your editor, create a new file called **server/main.ts**.

3. Add the imports at the top of the file:

    ```
    import { enableProdMode } from '@angular/core';
    import { NestFactory } from '@nestjs/core';
    import { Logger } from '@nestjs/common';
    import { ApplicationModule } from './app.module';
    ```

4. Define the constants that we will use in the server:

    ```
    const PORT = process.env.PORT || 8080;
    const HOST = process.env.HOST || '0.0.0.0';
    ```

5. Enable Angular production mode, as the server-side app will only run in production:

    ```
    enableProdMode();
    ```

6. Define the **bootstrap** function. This function creates a new instance of Nest based on our **ApplicationModule**, and starts the server by listening on the **HOST** and **PORT**:

    ```
    async function bootstrap() {
      const app = await NestFactory.create(ApplicationModule);
      await app.listen(PORT, HOST);
    }
    ```

7. The last step is to call the **bootstrap()** method we just defined. This returns a Promise, and in the **then()** block, we will log a friendly message with the URL where the server listens. We use the **catch()** block to log any errors:

```
bootstrap()
  .then(() => Logger.log('Server listening on http://${HOST}:${PORT}'))
  .catch(err => console.error(err));
```

```
main.ts  ✕

1   import { enableProdMode } from '@angular/core';
2   import { NestFactory } from '@nestjs/core';
3   import { Logger } from '@nestjs/common';
4   import { ApplicationModule } from './app.module';
5
6   const PORT = process.env.PORT || 8080;
7   const HOST = process.env.HOST || 'localhost';
8
9   enableProdMode();
10
11  async function bootstrap() {
12      const app = await NestFactory.create(ApplicationModule);
13      await app.listen(PORT, HOST);
14  }
15
16  bootstrap()
17      .then(() => Logger.log(`Server listening on http://${HOST}:${PORT}`))
18      .catch(err => console.error(err));
19
```

Figure 2.11: Implementing the Nest bootstrap file

Exercise 38: Implementing the Nest AppModule

In this exercise, we will create the **AppModule** that is bootstrapped by **main.ts**. We will decorate it with the **@Module()** decorator. Inside this decorator, we will import **AngularUniversalModule** and configure it by passing in the paths to the browser and server build of Angular. Follow these steps to complete this exercise:

1. In your editor, create a new file called **server/app.module.ts**.

2. Add the imports at the top of the file:

```
import { Module } from '@nestjs/common';
import { join } from 'path';
import { AngularUniversalModule, applyDomino } from '@nestjs/
ng-universal';
```

3. Define and export the **ApplicationModule** class:

```
export class ApplicationModule {}
```

4. Decorate the **ApplicationModule** class with the **@Module()** decorator:

```
@Module()
export class ApplicationModule {}
```

5. Pass an object in the decorator and set the value of the **imports** key to an array:

```
@Module({
  imports: [ ],
})
```

6. Add the **AngularUniversalModule** to the **imports** array and call the **forRoot()** method on it:

```
@Module({
  imports: [
    AngularUniversalModule.forRoot(),
  ],
})
```

7. Pass an object in the **forRoot()** method and define the **viewsPath** and **bundle** property with the correct paths:

```
AngularUniversalModule.forRoot({
  viewsPath: join(process.cwd(), 'dist/angular-social'),
  bundle: require('././../dist/angular-social-server/main.js'),
})
```

Exercise 39: Creating the WebPack Configuration

In this exercise, we will add a simple default WebPack configuration that comes with the Universal module from Nest. We will use this file to build our Nest server. Follow these steps to complete this exercise:

> **Note**
>
> This will package all of the dependencies into one file, so once we run the build step of Nest, we can simply package the **dist** folder and execute the app by running **node dist/server.js**.

1. Create a file called **webpack.config.js** in the project root and open it in the editor.

2. We will start with the imports:

    ```
    const webpack = require('webpack');
    const WebpackConfigFactory = require('@nestjs/ng-universal').
    WebpackConfigFactory;
    ```

3. Next, we will export an object that's created by calling **create** on the **WebpackConfigFactory** from Nest, and passing in **webpack**:

    ```
    module.exports = WebpackConfigFactory.create(webpack);
    ```

Exercise 40: Adding the Run Scripts to package.json

In this exercise, we will update **package.json** and add a script to build and start the server. Follow these steps to complete this exercise:

1. Open the **package.json** file from the root of our project in the editor.

2. Add the following keys to the **scripts** object:

    ```
    "build:nest": "webpack --config webpack.config.js --progress --colors",
    ```

3. Update the following keys in the **scripts** object:

    ```
    "start": "node ./dist/server",
    "build": "npm run build:browser && npm run build:server && npm run
    build:nest",
    ```

4. Open the terminal and run the complete build:

    ```
    $ npm run build
    ```

    ```
    > angular-social@0.0.0 build /Users/beeman/dev/angular-social
    > npm run build:browser && npm run build:server && npm run build:nest


    > angular-social@0.0.0 build:browser /Users/beeman/dev/angular-social
    > ng build angular-social --prod


    Date: 2018-09-28T08:52:40.461Z
    Hash: 4b5288e648fb41d6fa18
    Time: 15114ms
    chunk {0} runtime.80dbf10546ca9a40da1c.js (runtime) 2.23 kB [entry] [rendered]
    chunk {1} main.fcfab6d1b45e02bfbadd.js (main) 309 kB [initial] [rendered]
    chunk {2} polyfills.542e30e4ec0a2f0321ec.js (polyfills) 59.5 kB [initial] [rendered]
    chunk {3} styles.4fc469b3872a9e2acccc.css (styles) 178 bytes [initial] [rendered]
    chunk {4} 4.5ff9198407f5a779dc44.js () 5.59 kB  [rendered]

    > angular-social@0.0.0 build:server /Users/beeman/dev/angular-social
    > ng run angular-social:server:production


    Date: 2018-09-28T08:52:49.214Z
    Hash: 20d5de6a8db51cc4dbf0
    Time: 5552ms
    chunk {main} main.js, main.js.map (main) 118 kB [entry] [rendered]

    > angular-social@0.0.0 build:nest /Users/beeman/dev/angular-social
    > webpack --config webpack.config.js --progress --colors

    Hash: b395d5747147ac3cccfe
    Version: webpack 4.19.1
    Time: 9175ms
    Built at: 09/28/2018 3:52:59 AM
        Asset    Size  Chunks           Chunk Names
    server.js  6.78 MiB      0 [emitted]  server
    Entrypoint server = server.js
       [0] ./server/main.ts 3.29 KiB {0} [built]
     [203] ./src lazy namespace object 160 bytes {0} [built]
     [219] external "os" 42 bytes {0} [built]
     [222] external "crypto" 42 bytes {0} [built]
     [377] ./src sync 160 bytes {0} [built]
     [417] external "path" 42 bytes {0} [built]
     [419] external "fs" 42 bytes {0} [built]
     [425] external "events" 42 bytes {0} [built]
     [508] external "http" 42 bytes {0} [built]
     [509] external "https" 42 bytes {0} [built]
     [511] external "url" 42 bytes {0} [built]
     [607] external "querystring" 42 bytes {0} [built]
     [764] ./server/app.module.ts 1.19 KiB {0} [built]
     [769] external "timers" 42 bytes {0} [optional] [built]
     [839] ./dist/angular-social-server/main.js 115 KiB {0} [built]
        + 826 hidden modules
    → angular-social git:(master) x ▮
    ```

    Figure 2.12: Running the complete build

5. Start the server:

   ```
   $ npm start
   ```

```
→  angular-social git:(master) x npm start

> angular-social@0.0.0 start /Users/beeman/dev/angular-social
> node ./dist/server

[Nest] 74718   - 9/28/2018, 3:55:59 AM   [NestFactory] Starting Nest application...
(node:74718) [DEP0005] DeprecationWarning: Buffer() is deprecated due to security and usability issues. Please use
  the Buffer.alloc(), Buffer.allocUnsafe(), or Buffer.from() methods instead.
[Nest] 74718   - 9/28/2018, 3:55:59 AM   [InstanceLoader] ApplicationModule dependencies initialized +18ms
[Nest] 74718   - 9/28/2018, 3:55:59 AM   [InstanceLoader] AngularUniversalModule dependencies initialized +0ms
[Nest] 74718   - 9/28/2018, 3:55:59 AM   [NestApplication] Nest application successfully started +9ms
[Nest] 74718   - 9/28/2018, 3:55:59 AM   Server listening on http://localhost:8080 +4ms
```

Figure 2.13: Starting the server

6. Navigate to the server-side rendered build at **http://localhost:8080**.

7. Verify that the application works.

8. From the Chrome menu, select **View | Developer Tools | View Source** and verify that the application output gets rendered.

> **Note**
>
> If the page does not load properly, try loading it in an incognito window.

Adding Dynamic Metadata

Now that our pages can are rendered using server-side rendering, we can introduce new functionality to improve the app's behavior. At the moment, the app will still only display the default title set in **src/index.html**, and we won't have any other HTML meta tags added.

To enhance the SEO friendliness of our page, and to make sure that there is valuable information in our social preview, we want to address this.

Luckily, Angular comes with the **Meta** and **Title** classes, which allow us to add dynamic titles and metadata to our pages. When combined with server-side rendering, the metadata and page title will make sure that the pages that are indexed by the search engine have the proper meta tags set in the document header, and thus increase findability.

In this section, we will add a service that allows us to define this data, and we will update our container components to call in that service after the data is loaded from our resolvers.

Exercise 41: Creating the UiService

In this exercise, we will create the **UiService** and implement a method to update the metadata of a page rendered by Angular. Follow these steps to complete this exercise:

1. Open a terminal inside the project directory.

2. Run the following command to generate the **UiService** and register it in the **UiModule**:

   ```
   ng g s ui/services/ui --module ui/ui
   ```

   ```
   angular-social git:(master) ng g s ui/services/ui --module ui/ui
   CREATE src/app/ui/services/ui.service.spec.ts (350 bytes)
   CREATE src/app/ui/services/ui.service.ts (131 bytes)
   angular-social git:(master) x
   ```

   Figure 2.14: Creating the UiService

3. Open the **src/app/ui/services/ui.service.ts** file in your editor.

4. Add the following lines to the class definition:

   ```
   private appColor = '#C3002F';
   private appImage = '/assets/logo.svg';
   private appTitle = 'Angular Social';
   private appDescription = 'Angular Social is a Social Networking App built
   in Angular';
   ```

5. Import **Title** and **Meta** from **@angular/platform-browser**:

   ```
   import { Meta, Title } from '@angular/platform-browser'
   ```

6. Inject the **private title: Title** and **private meta: Meta** in the constructor:

   ```
   constructor(private meta: Meta, private title: Title) { }
   ```

7. Add a class method called **setMetaData** that takes in a **config** property:

   ```
   public setMetaData(config) {}
   ```

8. Add the following code to the body of the **setMetaData** property:

```
// Get the description from the config, or use the default App Description
const description = config.description || this.appDescription;

// Get the image from  the config or use the App Image;
const image = config.image || this.appImage;
// Get the title from  the config and append the App Title, or just use the
App Title
const title = config.title
  ? '${config.title} - ${this.appTitle}'
  : this.appTitle;

// Set the Application Title
this.title.setTitle(title);

// Add the Application Meta tags

const tags = [
  { name: 'description', content: description },
  { name: 'theme-color', content: this.appColor },
  { name: 'twitter:card', content: 'summary' },
  { name: 'twitter:image', content: image },
  { name: 'twitter:title', content: title },
  { name: 'twitter:description', content: description },
  { name: 'apple-mobile-web-app-capable', content: 'yes' },
  { name: 'apple-mobile-web-app-status-bar-style', content: 'black-
translucent' },
  { name: 'apple-mobile-web-app-title', content: title },
  { name: 'apple-touch-startup-image', content: image },
  { property: 'og:title', content: title },
  { property: 'og:description', content: description },
  { property: 'og:image', content: image },
];

tags.forEach(tag => this.meta.updateTag(tag));
```

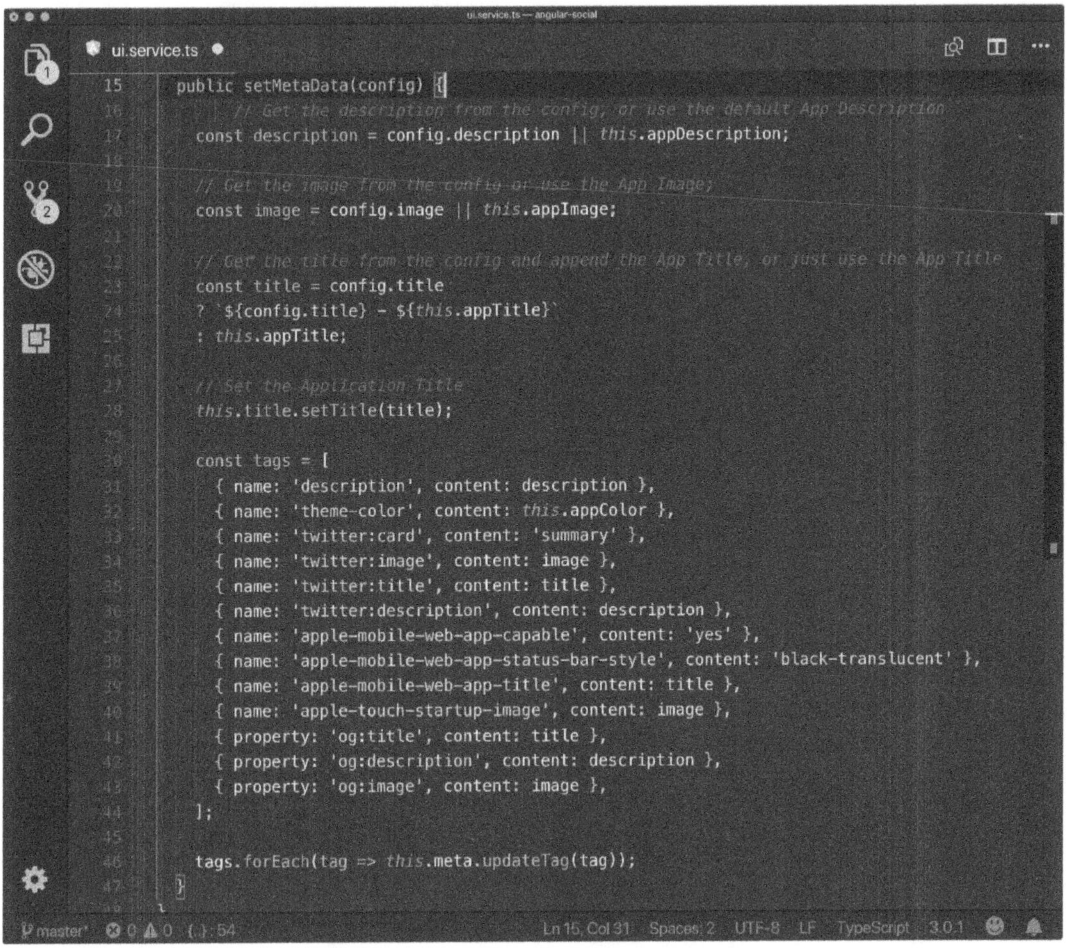

Figure 2.15: The setMetaData property

Our **UiService** is now ready to be used. We will start by adding it to the components in our next exercise.

Exercise 42: Adding Metadata to the PostListComponent

In this exercise, we will add the metadata to the **PostListComponent**. Follow these steps to complete this exercise:

1. Open the **src/app/post/containers/post-list/post-list.component.ts** file in your editor.

2. Add the **tap** operator to the import of **rxjs/operators**:

    ```
    import { map, tap } from 'rxjs/operators';
    ```

3. Import the **UiService**:

    ```
    import { UiService } from '../../../ui/services/ui.service';
    ```

4. Inside the constructor, inject **private ui: UiService**:

    ```
    constructor(private route: ActivatedRoute, public ui: UiService) { }
    ```

5. Add a class method called **setMetadata()** that accepts a **posts** property:

    ```
    setMetaData(posts: Post[]) {}
    ```

6. Add the following to the **setMetaData** method. In this method, we will construct the dynamic metadata that we will pass to our **setMetaData** method in the **UiService**:

    ```
    const description = 'Showing ${posts.length} posts';
    const title = 'Post List';
    this.ui.setMetaData({ description, title });
    ```

7. Add a new operator after the **map** operator in the **pipe** function in the **ngOnInit** method. This will pass the data we get from the API through the method we defined previously:

```
tap(posts => this.setMetaData(posts)),
```

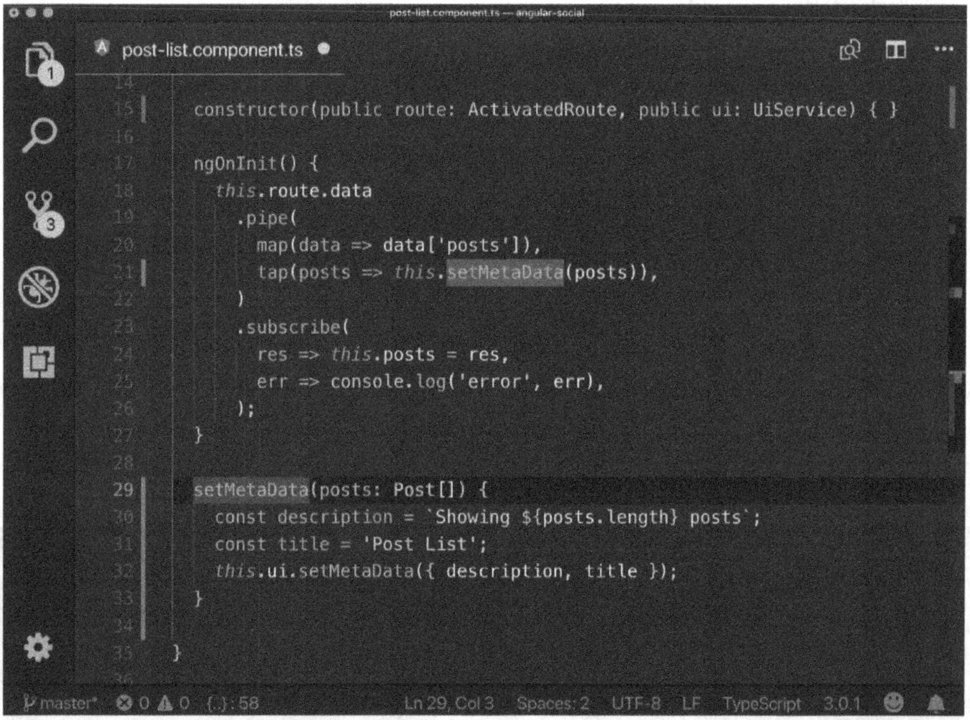

Figure 2.16: The post-list.component.ts file

Exercise 43: Adding Metadata to the PostDetailComponent

In this exercise, we will add the metadata to the **PostDetailComponent**. Follow these steps to complete this exercise:

1. Open the **src/app/post/containers/post-detail/post-detail.component.ts** file in your editor.

2. Add the **tap** operator to the import of **rxjs/operators**:

```
import { map, tap } from 'rxjs/operators';
```

3. Import the **UiService**:

```
import { UiService } from '../../../ui/services/ui.service';
```

4. Inside the constructor, inject **private ui: UiService**:

   ```
   constructor(private route: ActivatedRoute, private ui: UiService) { }
   ```

5. Add a class method called **setMetadata()** that accepts a **posts** property:

   ```
   setMetaData(post: Post) {}
   ```

6. Add the following to the **setMetaData** method. In this method, we will construct the dynamic metadata that we will pass to our **setMetaData** method in the **UiService**:

   ```
   setMetaData(post: Post) {
     const { date, profile, text } = post;
     const description = '${text} by ${profile.fullName}';
     const title = 'Post by ${profile.fullName} at ${date}';
     this.ui.setMetaData({ description, title });
   }
   ```

7. Update the **ngOnInit** method to the following code. This will pass the data we get from the API through the method we defined previously:

   ```
   tap(post => this.setMetaData(post))
   ```

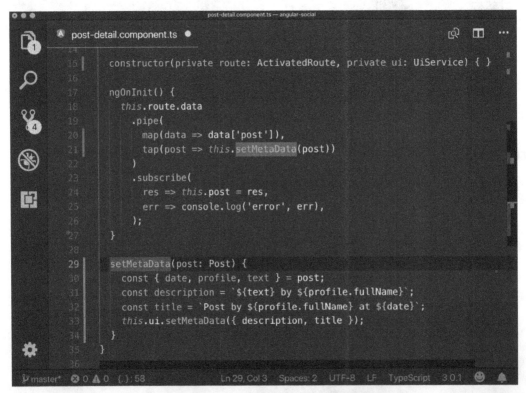

Figure 2.17: The post-detail.component.ts file

Now when you browse through the application, you should see that the title of the page updates, depending on the page you are visiting.

You can use the **Element Inspector** to verify that the metadata is being added to the rendered components:

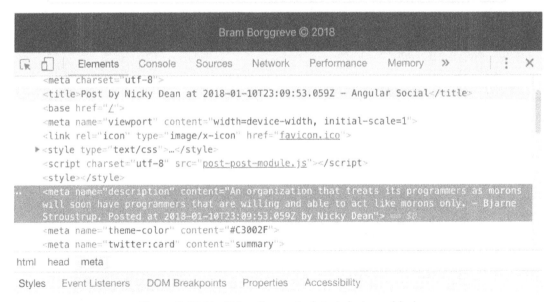

Figure 2.18: Verifying the metadata is being added

Deploying to Production

In this section, we will learn how to deploy a production version of the app to the cloud. A common way to deploy applications is using Docker. With Docker, you can create a container that holds and runs the app.

Docker containers are portable, so once they are built, they can run on different machines or platforms. We will deploy the app to **now.sh** using Docker. This will make the app available on the internet so that we can share it with others.

For information on how to install Docker, you can visit the Docker Getting Started website (https://docs.docker.com/v17.09/get-started/) or the official documentation (https://docs.docker.com/).

Exercise 44: Adding a Dockerfile to our Project

In this exercise, we will add a **Dockerfile** to our project. Follow these steps to complete this exercise:

1. Create a file called **Dockerfile** in the root of the project.

2. Add the following contents:

   ```
   FROM node:10-alpine

   RUN mkdir -p /app/dist
   WORKDIR /app
   COPY ./dist /app/dist

   EXPOSE 8080

   CMD [ "node", "dist/server" ]
   ```

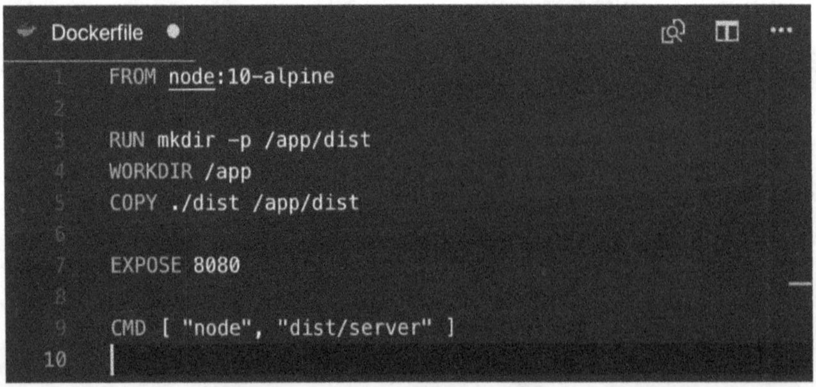

Figure 2.19: The Dockerfile

3. Add the following run scripts, which can be added to **package.json**:

```
"docker": "npm run docker:build && npm run docker:run",
"docker:build": "docker build -t angular-social:latest --rm .",
"docker:run": "docker run -it --rm -p 8080:8080 --name angular_social
angular-social:latest"
```

If we have access to Docker on our local machine, we can now simply run **npm run docker** and the container will be built and started, and will be accessible from **http://localhost:8080/**, but hosted on Docker.

If we don't have access to Docker on our local machine, we can deploy it to a cloud provider that supports Docker, such as now.sh (you can sign up for a free account if you don't have one already at https://zeit.co/now).

Exercise 45: Deploying our Docker Image to now.sh

Create an account on now.sh and download the **Now Desktop** (https://zeit.co/download) application. This should give you access to the **now** command-line parameter. Follow these steps to complete this exercise:

1. Create a file called **now.json** in the root of the project.

2. Add the following contents (and update the value of **alias** to something unique):

```
{
  "version": 1,
  "name": "angular-social",
  "alias": "angular-social",
  "type": "docker",
  "files": [
    "Dockerfile",
    "dist"
  ]
}
```

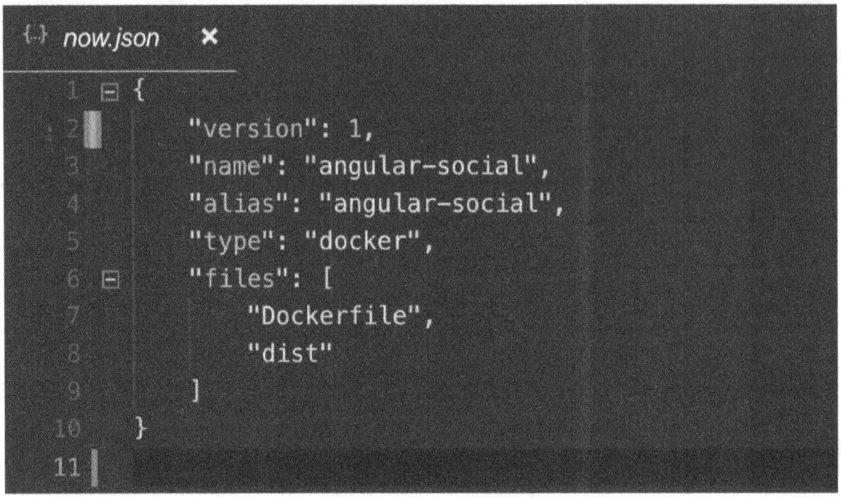

```json
{
    "version": 1,
    "name": "angular-social",
    "alias": "angular-social",
    "type": "docker",
    "files": [
        "Dockerfile",
        "dist"
    ]
}
```

Figure 2.20: The now.json file

3. Running the **now** command should deploy the application on now using Docker:

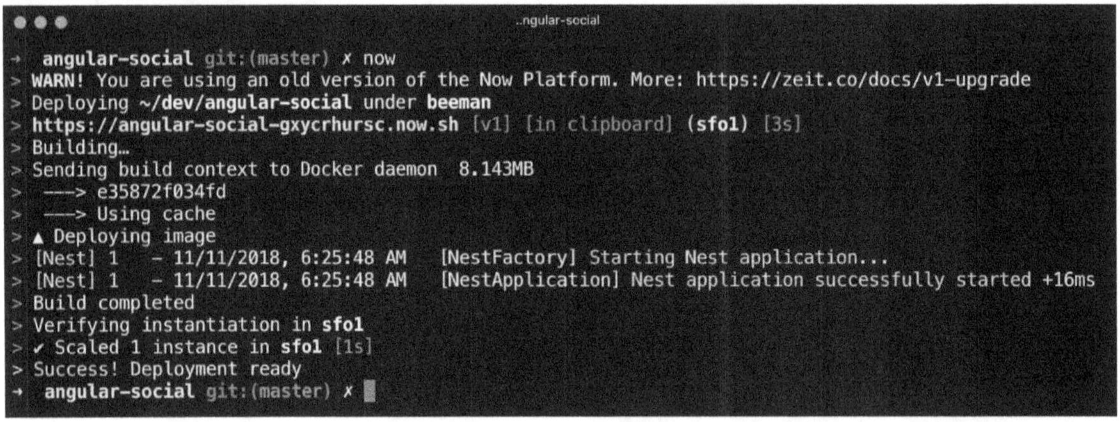

```
→  angular-social git:(master) ✗ now
> WARN! You are using an old version of the Now Platform. More: https://zeit.co/docs/v1-upgrade
> Deploying ~/dev/angular-social under beeman
> https://angular-social-gxycrhursc.now.sh [v1] [in clipboard] (sfo1) [3s]
> Building…
> Sending build context to Docker daemon  8.143MB
>   ---> e35872f034fd
>   ---> Using cache
> ▲ Deploying image
> [Nest] 1   - 11/11/2018, 6:25:48 AM   [NestFactory] Starting Nest application...
> [Nest] 1   - 11/11/2018, 6:25:48 AM   [NestApplication] Nest application successfully started +16ms
> Build completed
> Verifying instantiation in sfo1
> ✓ Scaled 1 instance in sfo1 [1s]
> Success! Deployment ready
→  angular-social git:(master) ✗
```

Figure 2.21: Running the now command

now will return a URL where the application will be hosted. You can use the **now alias** command to create an easy-to-remember name based on the value of **alias** in the config file, and use that URL to point to new deployments of the app and share it with others.

> **Note**
>
> The **alias** and other parameters of now can be stored in the object in **package. json**. Consider creating an entry in run scripts such as **"now": "now && now alias"** so that we can deploy the app by simply running **npm run now**.

Activity 9: Implementing the Transfer State Cache

Currently, when the server-side rendered app is loaded in the browser, there are two calls being made to the API. The first call is from when the page is rendered on the server. When it sends the complete page to the browser, Angular will start and make the request again. This is because the Angular app in the browser has no way of knowing it's started from a server-side rendered page.

To prevent this, we can cache the result of the API request on the server and send it along to the browser where it can be read. Luckily, there is a helper module for this that is very simple to implement.

The steps are as follows:

1. Import **TransferHttpCacheModule** from **@nguniversal/common** in **AppModule**.

2. Next, import **ServerTransferStateModule** from **@angular/platform-server** in **AppServerModule**.

Now when you create a new build of the app, you will only see that the API request gets made once.

If you view the source of the server-side rendered page, verify that you can see the application state as a snippet of JSON at the bottom of the page:

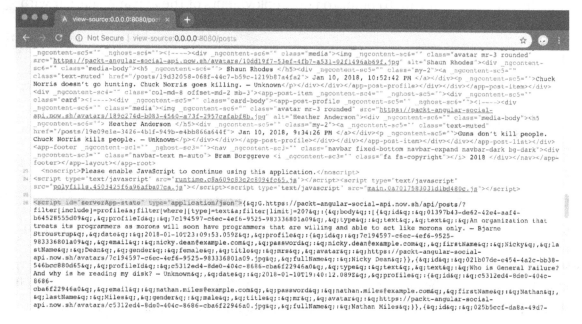

Figure 2.22: Viewing the source of the server-side rendered page

> **Note**
>
> The solution for this activity can be found on page 121.

Summary

In this chapter, we installed and configured Angular Universal and built a server using the NestJS framework. After that, we added support for dynamic metadata and a Docker configuration so that we could deploy our application to the cloud.

In the next chapter, we will configure service workers in our application.

3

Service Workers

Learning Objectives

By the end of the chapter, you will be able to:

- Add a service worker to the application

- Configure the service worker cache

- Test and debug the service worker

This chapter teaches us how to make our app into an Angular PWA and configure and test service workers for our app.

Introduction

In this chapter, we will add a service worker to the application that we built in the previous chapters.

We will add the Angular service worker module to our application and configure it to convert the app into a Progressive Web App.

What is a Service Worker?

A service worker is a script that the browser runs in the background that acts as a network proxy to manage network requests programmatically. It sits between the network and the device and caches content, enabling an offline experience for the user.

In addition to caching data, it can also synchronize API data in the background and add things such as push notifications.

What is a Progressive Web App?

A **Progressive Web App** (**PWA**) is a term that is used for web applications that behave similar to a native mobile application. Similar to native apps, they allow an application to be started when the user is offline, caching the UI elements and API calls to display an initial page. This way, a user can interact with the application on a basic level until the connection gets established. Once the connection is established, the PWA will retrieve the updated data from the server and refresh the application so that the user works with the latest data.

A great example of a famous progressive web is the Twitter mobile website (https://mobile.twitter.com/). A lot more can be found in this collection: https://pwa.rocks/.

> **Note**
>
> The official Angular documentation has a great section on service workers at https://angular.io/guide/service-worker-intro.

Installing Angular PWA

Angular comes with great support for service workers, and in recent versions, it has become super easy to set up. Whereas previously you had to manually install the dependencies, edit the Angular config, import a module, and configure it, you can now simply use the **ng add** command that got introduced in Angular CLI v6.

Exercise 46: Adding Angular PWA

In this exercise, we will add Angular PWA to our app. Follow these steps to complete this exercise:

1. Open the terminal in the project directory.

2. Install the necessary dependencies using the **npm** command:

    ```
    ng add @angular/pwa --project angular-social
    ```

3. When the installation is successful, we should see the new package added to the **dependencies** object in our project's **package.json** file.

Let's move on to the next section, where we will enable the service worker in the application.

Configuring the Service Worker

In the previous section, we added the service worker configuration file, **src/ngsw-config.json**, to our project, but we have not configured anything yet.

In this section, we will add two types of configuration, **asset groups** and **data groups**. We will use a fairly straightforward configuration for our service worker. Please refer to the service worker configuration page for a detailed description of the configuration options in **ngsw-config.json**.

Exercise 47: Configuring Asset Groups

In this exercise, we will append two items to the asset groups configuration. In the asset groups configuration, we will specify how we want our service worker to handle the assets of the application.

When we talk about assets, we think of stylesheets, images, and external JS files. The first asset group caches the data that comes from the domains that we use to fetch our CSS and the fonts included in that CSS. The second asset group caches the static data from the API we work with, in this case, the user avatars:

1. Open the **src/ngsw-config.json** file in your editor.

2. Locate the **assetGroups** array.

3. Add the following two objects to this array:

```json
{
  "name": "externals",
  "installMode": "prefetch",
  "updateMode": "prefetch",
  "resources": {
    "urls": [
      "https://ajax.googleapis.com/**",
      "https://fonts.googleapis.com/**",
      "https://fonts.gstatic.com/**",
      "https://maxcdn.bootstrapcdn.com/**"
    ]
  }
},
{
  "name": "avatars",
  "installMode": "prefetch",
  "updateMode": "prefetch",
  "resources": {
    "urls": [
      "http://localhost:3000/avatars/**",
      "https://packt-angular-social.now.sh/avatars/**"
    ]
  }
}
```

4. Make sure to correctly format the JSON. Use https://jsonlint.com/ to make sure.

Exercise 48: Configuring Data Groups

In this exercise, we create the data groups configuration.

In the data groups configuration, we must specify how we want our service worker to cache the data of the APIs we are requesting data from. We must define one data group that caches the requests from our API.

Follow these steps to complete this exercise:

1. Open the **src/ngsw-config.json** file in your editor.

2. Create a top-level array with the **dataGroups** key.

3. Add the following object to this array:

```
{
  "name": "rest-api",
  "urls": [
    "http://localhost:3000/api/**",
    "https://packt-angular-social.now.sh/api/**"
  ],
  "cacheConfig": {
    "strategy": "freshness",
    "maxSize": 100,
    "maxAge": "1h",
    "timeout": "5s"
  }
}
```

The complete content of **src/ngsw-config.json** should look like this:

```
{
  "index": "/index.html",
  "assetGroups": [
    {
      "name": "app",
      "installMode": "prefetch",
      "resources": {
        "files": [
          "/favicon.ico",
          "/index.html",
          "/*.css",
          "/*.js"
        ]
      }
    }
```

```json
      }, {
        "name": "assets",
        "installMode": "lazy",
        "updateMode": "prefetch",
        "resources": {
          "files": [
            "/assets/**"
          ]
        }
      },
      {
        "name": "externals",
        "installMode": "prefetch",
        "updateMode": "prefetch",
        "resources": {
          "urls": [
            "https://ajax.googleapis.com/**",
            "https://fonts.googleapis.com/**",
            "https://fonts.gstatic.com/**",
            "https://maxcdn.bootstrapcdn.com/**"
          ]
        }
      },
      {
        "name": "avatars",
        "installMode": "prefetch",
        "updateMode": "prefetch",
        "resources": {
          "urls": [
            "http://localhost:3000/avatars/**",
            "https://packt-angular-social.now.sh/avatars/**"
          ]
        }
      }
    ],
    "dataGroups": [
      {
```

```
      "name": "rest-api",
      "urls": [
        "http://localhost:3000/api/**",
        "https://packt-angular-social.now.sh/api/**"
      ],
      "cacheConfig": {
        "strategy": "freshness",
        "maxSize": 100,
        "maxAge": "1h",
        "timeout": "5s"
      }
    }
  ]
}
```

We have now configured the asset groups and data groups of the application in our service worker.

With this configuration and our service worker running, we should be able to retrieve a fully styled application that displays the latest API data.

> **Note**
>
> Refer to the Angular service worker configuration page at https://angular.io/guide/service-worker-config for a detailed description of the configuration options in `ngsw-config.json`.

Testing the Service Worker

In this section, we will see how we can test our service worker.

Checking Where the Data Comes From

Using the Chrome Developer Tools, it's easy to see where a particular resource is being retrieved from.

Using the **Network** tab in Chrome Developer Tools, you can see what files are being retrieved, where the data comes from, and how long it took the browser to fetch those resources. This following screenshot shows a *normal* page request, where each of the files are downloaded from the web server:

Name	Status	Type	Initiator	Size	Time	Waterfall
localhost	200	document	Other	1.0 KB	3 ms	
styles.4fc469b3872a9e2acccc.css	200	stylesheet	(index)	459 B	4 ms	
runtime.f6c7a82a00e9e6b66a52.js	200	script	(index)	2.5 KB	4 ms	
polyfills.542e30e4ec0a2f0321ec.js	200	script	(index)	58.4 KB	5 ms	
main.26e23d1c54b7b2fd24b6.js	200	script	(index)	313 KB	7 ms	
bootstrap.min.css	200	stylesheet	(index)	21.0 KB	320 ms	
font-awesome.min.css	200	stylesheet	(index)	7.3 KB	324 ms	
4.cf3e55ee54045cddfcc3.js	200	script	runtime.f6c7a82...js:1	7.2 KB	3 ms	
?filter[include]=profile&filter[where][type]=text&filter[im...	200	xhr	polyfills.542e30e...js:1	3.2 KB	842 ms	
7c194597-c6ec-4ef6-9525-983336801a09.jpg	200	jpeg	main.26e23d1...js:1	3.1 KB	614 ms	
c5312ed4-8de0-404c-8686-cba6f22946a0.jpg	200	jpeg	main.26e23d1...js:1	5.1 KB	549 ms	
888aec66-9ba5-4bc5-954c-2edab96a0ba2.jpg	200	jpeg	main.26e23d1...js:1	6.2 KB	633 ms	
c83b1e6e-e67d-4f6b-a120-f7faf7ae6371.jpg	200	jpeg	main.26e23d1...js:1	5.8 KB	598 ms	
fd08444e-ec1a-4001-8ae0-452214e7db8d.jpg	200	jpeg	main.26e23d1...js:1	11.3 KB	605 ms	
4e2a177a-d197-4148-8c1e-dde93231fa26.jpg	200	jpeg	main.26e23d1...js:1	6.9 KB	553 ms	
613f3aa5-5bd0-40bd-b156-5b53fc6664e5.jpg	200	jpeg	main.26e23d1...js:1	5.1 KB	558 ms	
27839415-c3f7-4ef2-bedd-264497f6d14a.jpg	200	jpeg	main.26e23d1...js:1	3.9 KB	525 ms	
189c274d-b083-4560-a73f-2957cafabf8b.jpg	200	jpeg	main.26e23d1...js:1	4.0 KB	543 ms	
38bbb7ac-d244-43e4-9bb4-78579591e193.jpg	200	jpeg	main.26e23d1...js:1	4.1 KB	539 ms	
38fce289-85bf-46e1-aa3c-8ef3bef685fb.jpg	200	jpeg	main.26e23d1...js:1	5.9 KB	529 ms	
e9b0ebd1-e278-4dc2-bedb-7e1e9320d6ec.jpg	200	jpeg	main.26e23d1...js:1	5.2 KB	576 ms	
10dd19f7-53ef-4fb7-a531-02f1496ab69f.jpg	200	jpeg	main.26e23d1...js:1	3.3 KB	535 ms	
5385775d-49ee-4b1e-ada7-8e0d9f9e9dc0.jpg	200	jpeg	main.26e23d1...js:1	3.7 KB	531 ms	
logo.svg	200	svg+xml	main.26e23d1...js:1	1.1 KB	3 ms	
fontawesome-webfont.woff2?v=4.7.0	200	font	Other	75.8 KB	374 ms	
ngsw-worker.js	200	javascript	ngsw-worker.js	0 B	5 ms	
ngsw.json?ngsw-cache-bust=0.9331129880609661	200	fetch	ngsw-worker.js:2637	3.7 KB	2 ms	
4.cf3e55ee54045cddfcc3.js	200	fetch	ngsw-worker.js:742	(from disk cache)	0 ms	

Figure 3.1: A normal page request

In the following screenshot, you can see in the **Size** column that the data is retrieved from the service worker. This means that it did not make a request to the network to fetch those items; instead, it got it from the browser cache:

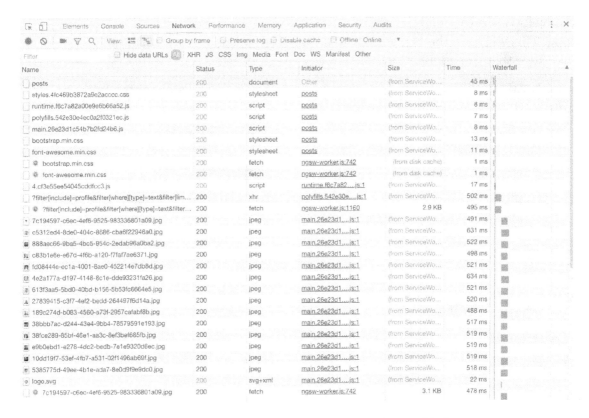

Figure 3.2: A page request with service worker enabled

Enabling Offline Mode

It's in the nature of a web browser to be online, but in reality, we've all found ourselves in situations where our device is offline due to a lack of network connectivity.

To develop apps that can handle these situations, Chrome offers a so-called **offline mode**. This will stop the browser from connecting to the network. This way, we can make sure that the application behaves as expected.

In the **Network** tab in Chrome Developer Tools, you can find a checkbox with the word **Offline**, which triggers this behavior:

Figure 3.3: The Network tab

After checking this box, you will see a yellow indicator next to the tab name that indicates that there is something unusual going on with the **Network** tab.

Figure 3.4: Offline option enabled

Exercise 49: Building and Running the App

In this exercise, we will build a production version of the app, which enables the service worker. Once the build is made, we will host the build using a simple web server called **serve** and open it in our browser. Follow these steps to complete this exercise:

1. Build the browser app using the following command:

    ```
    npm run build:browser
    ```

2. Serve the app using the command:

```
npx serve -s ./dist/angular-social
```

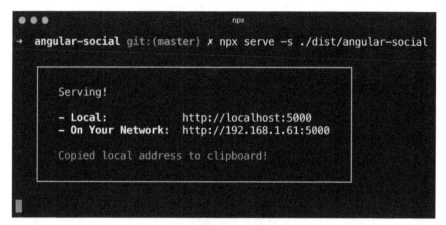

Figure 3.5: Serving the app

3. The application will now be served on **http://localhost:5000**.

4. Open the page in the browser. You should see the list of posts:

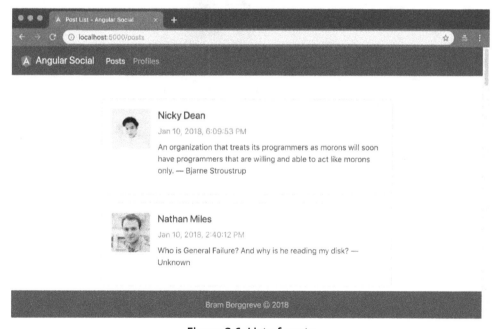

Figure 3.6: List of posts

5. Open the **Console** tab in Chrome Developer Tools and verify that there are no errors.

Exercise 50: Verifying that the Service Worker is Active

In this exercise, we will see how the app behaves when the service worker is enabled. Follow these steps to complete this exercise:

1. Open the page from the last exercise in your browser.

2. Open the **Network** tab in Chrome Developer Tools.

3. With this **Network** tab open, navigate to **http://localhost:5000** to see where the data comes from.

    You should see that the data gets loaded from the service worker:

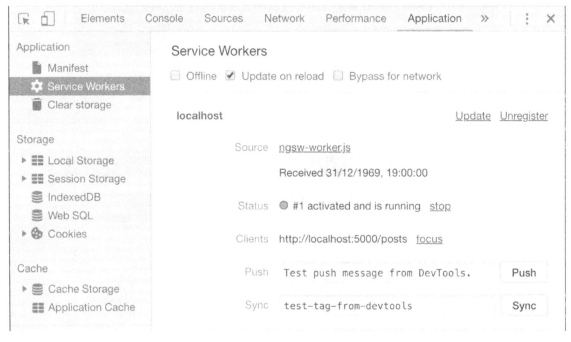

Figure 3.7: Service worker is active

Exercise 51: Running the Application in Offline Mode

In this exercise, we will set the application to offline mode and verify that the service worker displays a complete and cached version of the app. Follow these steps to complete this exercise:

1. Open the page from the last exercise in your browser.

2. Open the **Network** tab in Chrome Developer Tools.

3. Enable offline mode by using the **Offline** checkbox.

4. While in offline mode, navigate to `http://localhost:5000`.

   You should see that the application still gets loaded and that it displays cached data.

Debugging the Service Worker

There is a famous saying in computer science:

"There are two hard problems in computer science: cache invalidation and naming things"

- Phil Karlton

The first one applies to debugging service workers. As discussed earlier, a service worker adds a caching layer between the network and the device. This inherently makes it hard to debug because when you update your service worker definition or the configuration of your website, your changes might very well be cached and thus not visible.

This is quite a well-known challenge while developing application with service worker support, so it's good to understand how to debug the service worker.

Angular provides several mechanisms for deactivating a service worker in case of unexpected behavior. These mechanisms are described in the *Service Worker Safety* section of the service worker documentation at https://angular.io/guide/service-worker-devops#service-worker-safety.

Chrome Developer Tools to the Rescue

Chrome Developer Tools is an advanced tool for inspecting and debugging the technology behind websites, and luckily it has great support for service workers.

In the **Application** tab, we can see which service workers are installed, what their status is, and unregister them to make sure that we download the latest version.

Exercise 52: Verifying that the Service Worker is Running

In this exercise, we will locate where we can find the running service worker. Follow these steps to complete this exercise:

1. Open the page from the last exercise in your browser.

2. Open the **Application** tab in Chrome Developer Tools.

3. In the sidebar of the **Application** tab, click on the **Service Workers** link.

4. Verify that there is an entry in the list of service workers.

5. Verify that the status of the service worker is **activated and is running**:

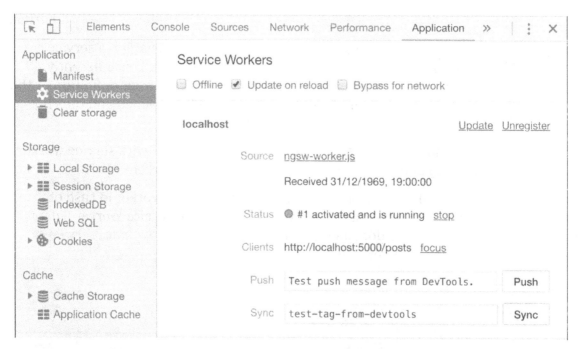

Figure 3.8: Service worker active and running

Exercise 53: Unregistering the Service Worker

In this exercise, we will unregister our service worker. Follow these steps to complete this exercise:

1. Open the page from the last exercise in your browser.

2. Open the **Application** tab in Chrome Developer Tools and click the **Service Workers** link in the sidebar.

3. Locate the entry of the service worker that has the **Status** set to **activated**.

4. Click the **Unregister** link next to the **Update** link.

5. The status of the service worker will change to **activated and is stopped**.

6. When you now refresh the page, a new service worker should be loaded:

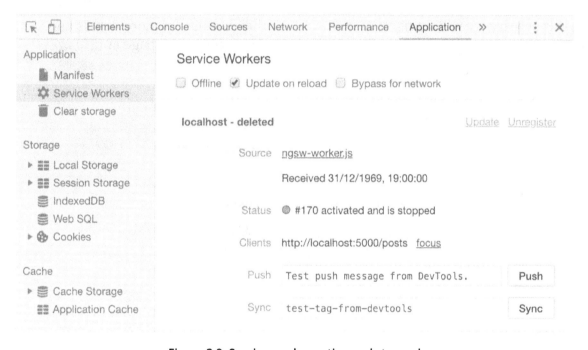

Figure 3.9: Service worker active and stopped

> **Note**
>
> Note that if you just refresh the page, it will load the same service worker from our build.

The development cycle for building a service worker looks something like this:

1. Make a change in the Angular application.

2. Create a production build (`npm run build:browser`).

3. Serve the new build (`npx http-server ./dist/browser`).

4. Unregister the currently active service worker.

5. Browse to the new version and verify that the changes you made are applied.

Activity 10: Communicating with the Service Worker

In the `@angular/service-worker` package, we can find the `SwPush` and `SwUpdate` services. These services contain ways to communicate with the service worker, relatively for sending push messages and checking for new updates of the service worker.

In this activity, we will simply load them and log their status. For more details and techniques, you can refer to the *Service Worker Communications* page at https:// angular.io/guide/service-worker-communications.

The steps are as follows:

1. Open the `src/app/app.module.ts` file in your editor.

2. Import `SwPush` and `SwUpdate` from `@angular/service-worker`.

3. Add a constructor and inject `SwPush` and `SwUpdate`.

4. Add the following lines in the constructor method:

```
console.log('Push enabled: ', push.isEnabled);
console.log('Updated enabled: ', updates.isEnabled);
```

Now, when you create a new build of the app, verify that you can see a message being printed in the console that tells the status of the **SwPush** and **SwUpdate** classes:

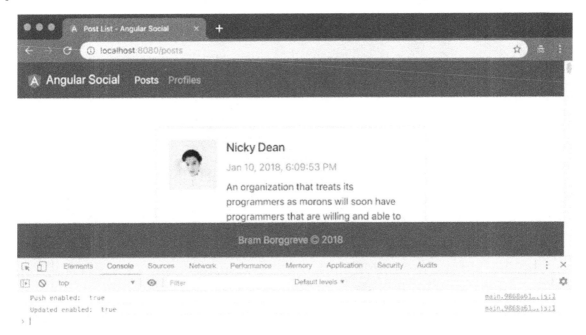

Figure 3.10: SwPush and SwUpdate messages in the console

> **Note**
>
> The solution for this activity can be found on page 122.

Summary

In this chapter, we used **ng add** to add a service worker to the application. We then configured the service worker and tested its behavior using Chrome Developer Tools. Lastly, we looked at how to debug the service worker.

In this book, we have built an app from scratch using Angular CLI. We used the Bootstrap framework to create a reusable user interface and added a module to list data that comes from an API.

Once this basic application was working, we added support for server-side rendering. We installed and configured Angular Universal and built a server using the NestJS framework. After that, we added support for dynamic metadata and a Docker configuration so that we could deploy it to the cloud. We completed the app by adding and configuring a service worker so that it could work as a Progressive Web App.

Appendix A

About

This section is included to assist the students to perform the activities in the book.
It includes detailed steps that are to be performed by the students to achieve the objectives of
the activities.

Chapter 1: Creating the Base Application

Activity 1: Using a BootSwatch Theme

Solution:

1. Navigate to BootSwatch Themes (https://www.bootstrapcdn.com/bootswatch/) on BootstrapCDN.

2. Select one of the themes and copy the link to the CSS:

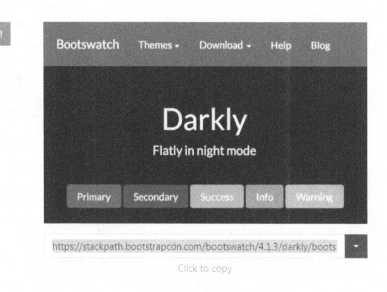

Figure 1.31: Selecting the Darkly theme

3. Update the link to Bootstrap CSS in **src/styles.css**:

```
@import url('https://stackpath.bootstrapcdn.com/bootswatch/4.1.3/darkly/
bootstrap.min.css');
```

4. Refresh the app in the browser and verify that the theme has been updated:

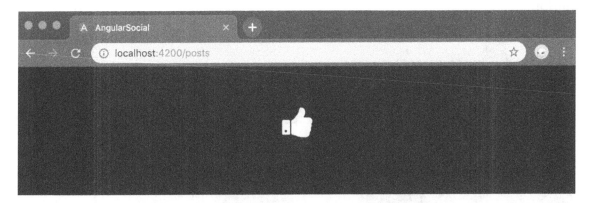

Figure 1.32: Thumbs-up icon in the Darkly theme

Activity 2: Using Different Font Awesome Icons

Solution:

1. Open the **src/app/app.component.html** file.

2. Navigate to the Font Awesome icon list at https://fontawesome.com/v4.7.0/icons/.

3. Replace the value of **fa-thumbs-up** with another icon. Note that you always need the **fa** class:

```
<i class="fa fa-trash"></i>
```

4. Refresh the app in the browser and verify that the browser now shows your new icon:

Figure 1.33: The trash icon

Activity 3: Moving the Header to a Separate Component

Solution:

1. Create a component called **HeaderComponent**:

   ```
   ng g c ui/components/header
   ```

2. Use the selector to reference the **HeaderComponent** from the **LayoutComponent**.

3. Move the header markup from **layout.component.html** to **header.component.html**:

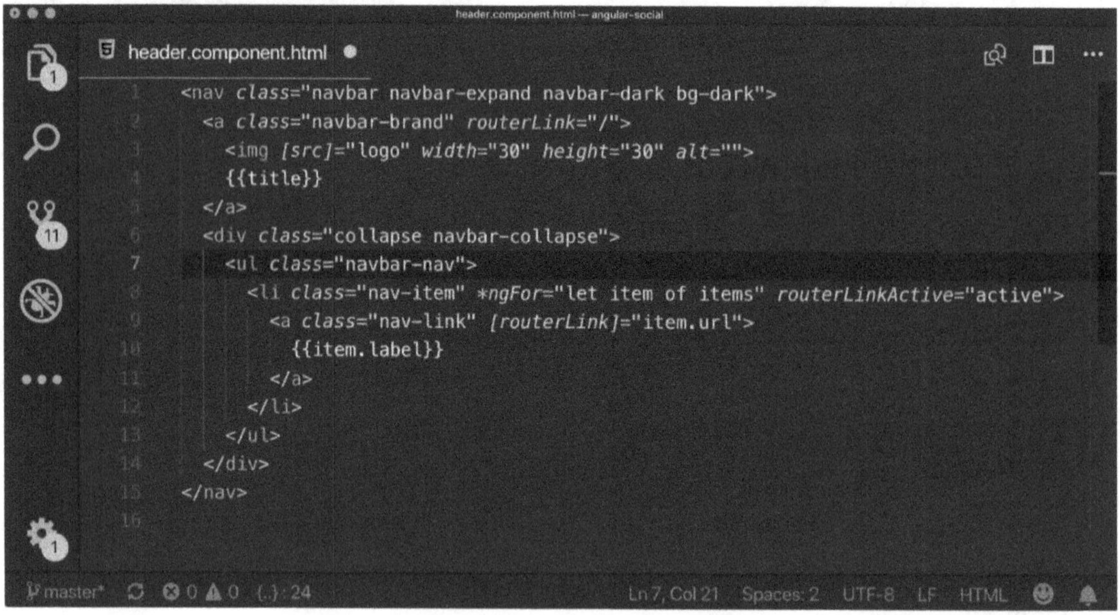

Figure 1.34: The header.component.html file

4. Move the header class properties from **layout.component.ts** to **header.component.ts**:

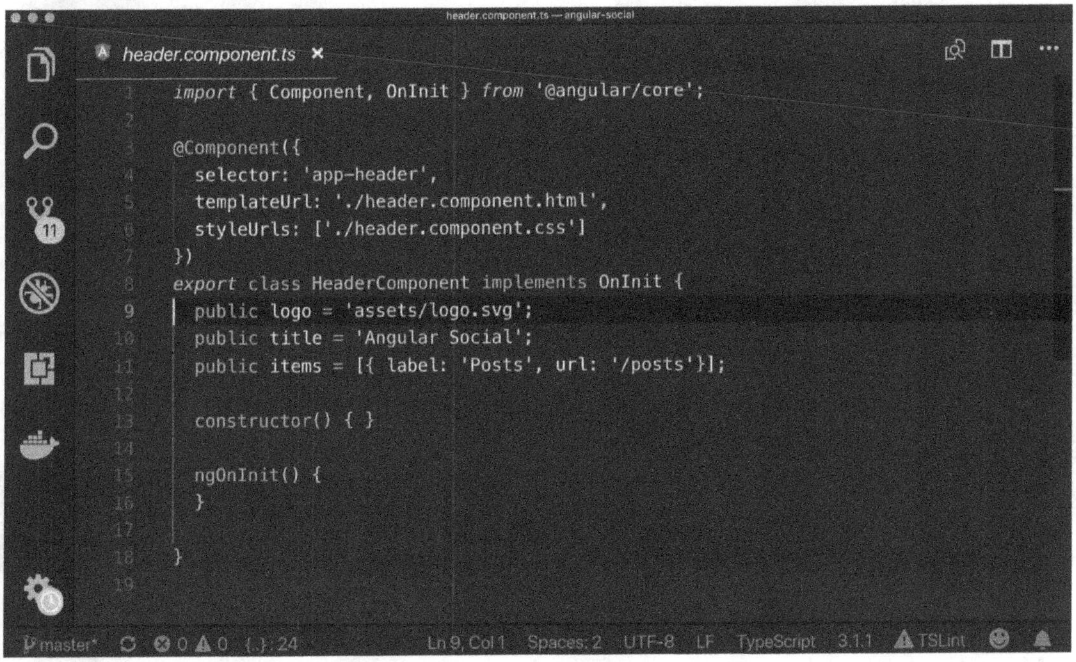

Figure 1.35: The header.component.ts file

Activity 4: Moving the Footer to a Separate Component

Solution:

1. Create a component called **FooterComponent**:

   ```
   ng g c ui/components/footer
   ```

2. Use the selector to reference the **FooterComponent** from the **LayoutComponent**.

3. Move the footer markup from `layout.component.html` to `footer.component.html`:

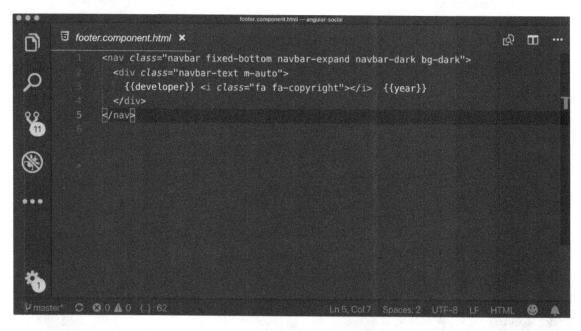

```
<nav class="navbar fixed-bottom navbar-expand navbar-dark bg-dark">
  <div class="navbar-text m-auto">
    {{developer}} <i class="fa fa-copyright"></i>  {{year}}
  </div>
</nav>
```

Figure 1.36: The footer.component.html file

4. Move the footer class properties from `layout.component.ts` to `footer.component.ts`:

```
import { Component, OnInit } from '@angular/core';

@Component({
  selector: 'app-footer',
  templateUrl: './footer.component.html',
  styleUrls: ['./footer.component.css']
})
export class FooterComponent implements OnInit {
  public developer = 'Bram Borggreve';
  public year = '2018';

  constructor() { }

  ngOnInit() {
  }

}
```

Figure 1.37: The footer.component.ts file

Activity 5: Creating a ProfileModule

Solution:

1. Create a module called **ProfileModule** using the following command:

```
ng g m profile --routing
```

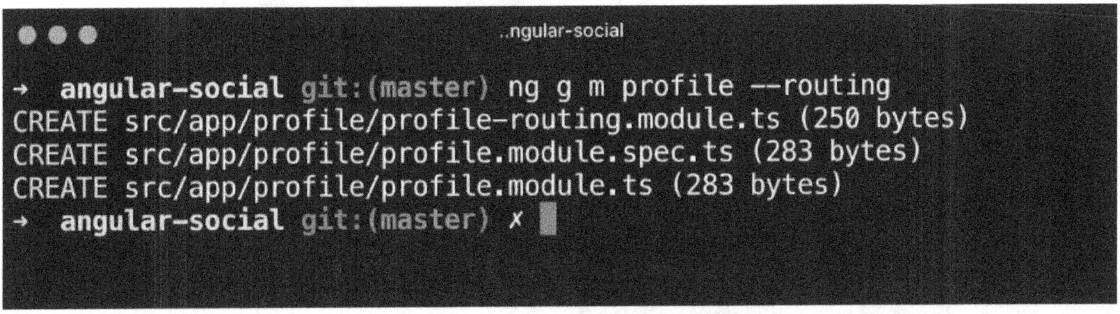

Figure 1.38: Creating the ProfileModule

2. Define the **/profiles/** route to lazy load this new module in **app-routing.module. ts**:

```
{
  path: 'profiles',
  loadChildren: './profile/profile.module#ProfileModule',
},
```

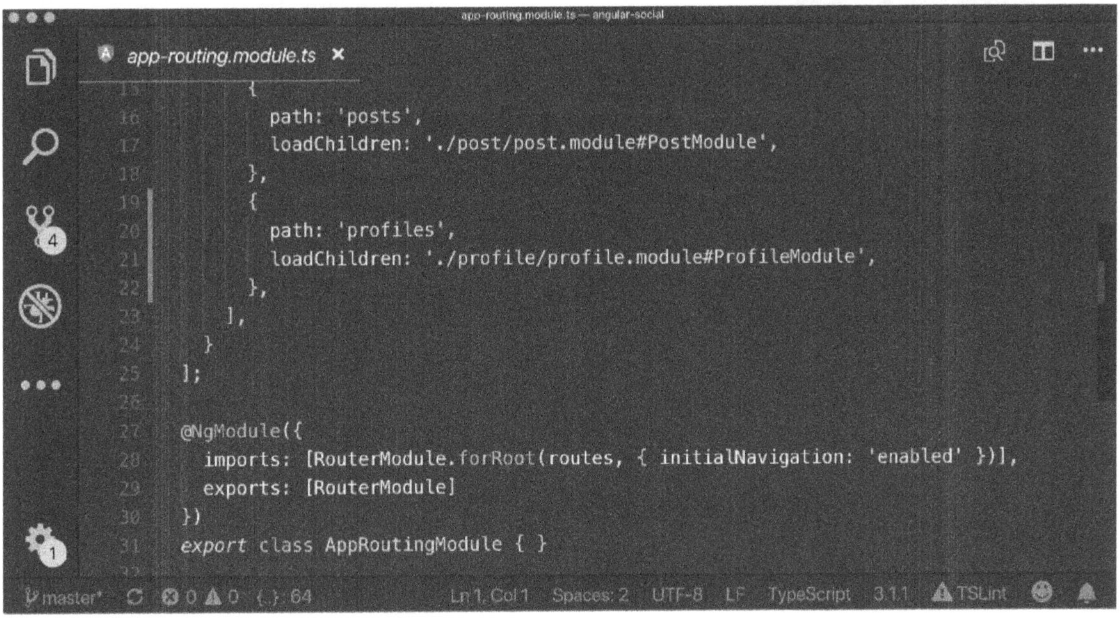

Figure 1.39: Defining the /profiles/ route

3. Add a menu item to link to the **/profiles/** URL in the `header.component.ts` file created in *Activity* 3, as shown here:

```
public items = [
    { label: 'Posts', url: '/posts'},
    { label: 'Profiles', url: '/profiles'},
];
```

Figure 1.40: Defining the /profiles/ URL

The final output will be as follows:

Figure 1.41: The Profiles menu item

Activity 6: Creating Container Components

Solution:

1. Add the `ProfileListComponent` and `ProfileDetailComponent` containers using the following commands:

```
ng g c profile/containers/profile-list
ng g c profile/containers/profile-detail
```

```
→ angular-social git:(master) x ng g c profile/containers/profile-list
CREATE src/app/profile/containers/profile-list/profile-list.component.css (0 bytes)
CREATE src/app/profile/containers/profile-list/profile-list.component.html (31 bytes)
CREATE src/app/profile/containers/profile-list/profile-list.component.spec.ts (664 bytes)
CREATE src/app/profile/containers/profile-list/profile-list.component.ts (292 bytes)
UPDATE src/app/profile/profile.module.ts (392 bytes)
→ angular-social git:(master) x ng g c profile/containers/profile-detail
CREATE src/app/profile/containers/profile-detail/profile-detail.component.css (0 bytes)
CREATE src/app/profile/containers/profile-detail/profile-detail.component.html (33 bytes)
CREATE src/app/profile/containers/profile-detail/profile-detail.component.spec.ts (678 byte
s)
CREATE src/app/profile/containers/profile-detail/profile-detail.component.ts (300 bytes)
UPDATE src/app/profile/profile.module.ts (511 bytes)
→ angular-social git:(master) x
```

Figure 1.42: Creating the container components

2. Add routes to the container components in **ProfileRoutingModule**, as shown in the following screenshot:

```typescript
import { NgModule } from '@angular/core';
import { Routes, RouterModule } from '@angular/router';
import { ProfileListComponent } from './containers/profile-list/profile-list.component';
import { ProfileDetailComponent } from './containers/profile-detail/profile-detail.component';

const routes: Routes = [
  {
    path: '',
    component: ProfileListComponent,
  },
  {
    path: ':id',
    component: ProfileDetailComponent,
  },
];

@NgModule({
  imports: [RouterModule.forChild(routes)],
  exports: [RouterModule]
})
export class ProfileRoutingModule { }
```

Figure 1.43: Adding routes

Activity 7: Creating Service and Resolvers

Solution:

1. Add a **ProfileService** to retrieve the data:

```
ng g s profile/services/profile
```

```
→  angular-social git:(master) ng g s profile/services/profile
CREATE src/app/profile/services/profile.service.spec.ts (338 bytes)
CREATE src/app/profile/services/profile.service.ts (136 bytes)
→  angular-social git:(master) x ng g class profile/resolvers/profile-resolver
CREATE src/app/profile/resolvers/profile-resolver.ts (33 bytes)
→  angular-social git:(master) x ng g class profile/resolvers/profiles-resolver
CREATE src/app/profile/resolvers/profiles-resolver.ts (34 bytes)
→  angular-social git:(master) x ng g class profile/model/profile
CREATE src/app/profile/model/profile.ts (25 bytes)
→  angular-social git:(master) x
```

Figure 1.44: Creating the ProfileService

2. Add **ProfilesResolver** and **ProfileResolver**:

```
ng g class profile/resolvers/profile-resolver
ng g class profile/resolvers/profiles-resolver
ng g class profile/model/profile
```

Use them in the **ProfileRoutingModule**, as shown in the following screenshot:

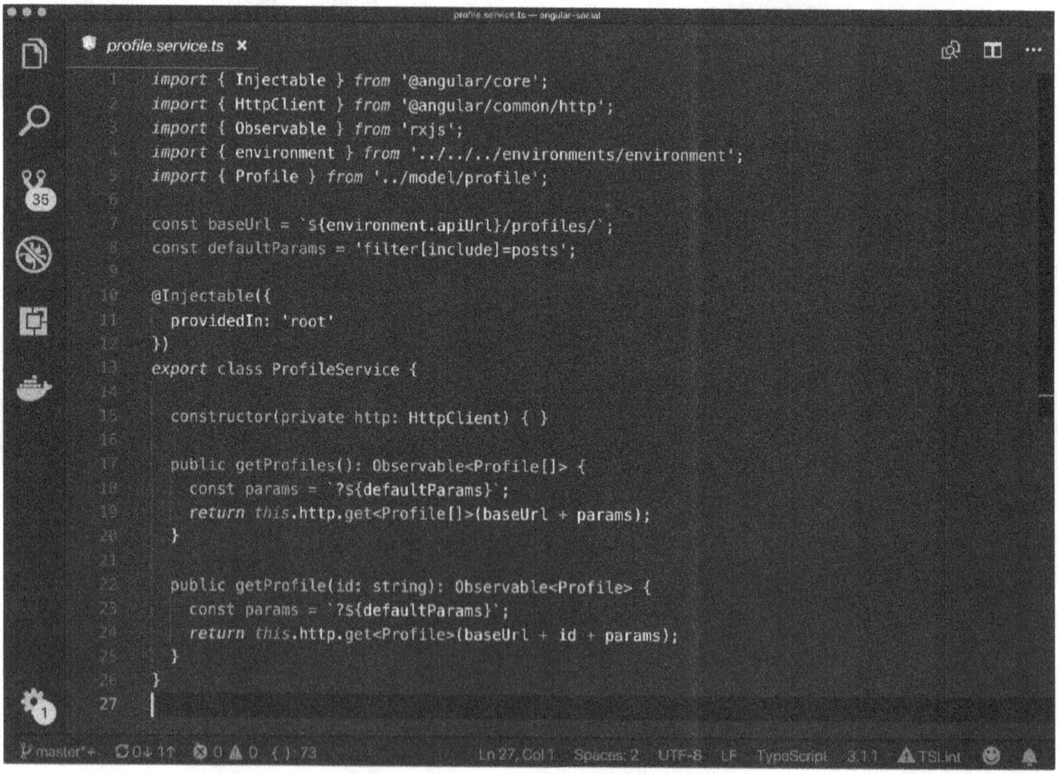

```typescript
import { Injectable } from '@angular/core';
import { HttpClient } from '@angular/common/http';
import { Observable } from 'rxjs';
import { environment } from '../../../environments/environment';
import { Profile } from '../model/profile';

const baseUrl = `${environment.apiUrl}/profiles/`;
const defaultParams = 'filter[include]=posts';

@Injectable({
  providedIn: 'root'
})
export class ProfileService {

  constructor(private http: HttpClient) { }

  public getProfiles(): Observable<Profile[]> {
    const params = `?${defaultParams}`;
    return this.http.get<Profile[]>(baseUrl + params);
  }

  public getProfile(id: string): Observable<Profile> {
    const params = `?${defaultParams}`;
    return this.http.get<Profile>(baseUrl + id + params);
  }
}
```

Figure 1.45: the ProfileRoutingModule

Activity 8: Creating Presentational Components

Solution:

1. Create the **ProfileItemComponent** and the **ProfilePostComponent**:

   ```
   ng g c profile/components/profile-item
   ng g c profile/components/profile-post
   ```

```
● ● ●                              ..ngular-social
→  angular-social git:(master) x ng g c profile/components/profile-item
CREATE src/app/profile/components/profile-item/profile-item.component.css (0 bytes)
CREATE src/app/profile/components/profile-item/profile-item.component.html (31 bytes)
CREATE src/app/profile/components/profile-item/profile-item.component.spec.ts (664 bytes)
CREATE src/app/profile/components/profile-item/profile-item.component.ts (292 bytes)
UPDATE src/app/profile/profile.module.ts (622 bytes)
→  angular-social git:(master) x ng g c profile/components/profile-post
CREATE src/app/profile/components/profile-post/profile-post.component.css (0 bytes)
CREATE src/app/profile/components/profile-post/profile-post.component.html (31 bytes)
CREATE src/app/profile/components/profile-post/profile-post.component.spec.ts (664 bytes)
CREATE src/app/profile/components/profile-post/profile-post.component.ts (292 bytes)
UPDATE src/app/profile/profile.module.ts (733 bytes)
→  angular-social git:(master) x █
```

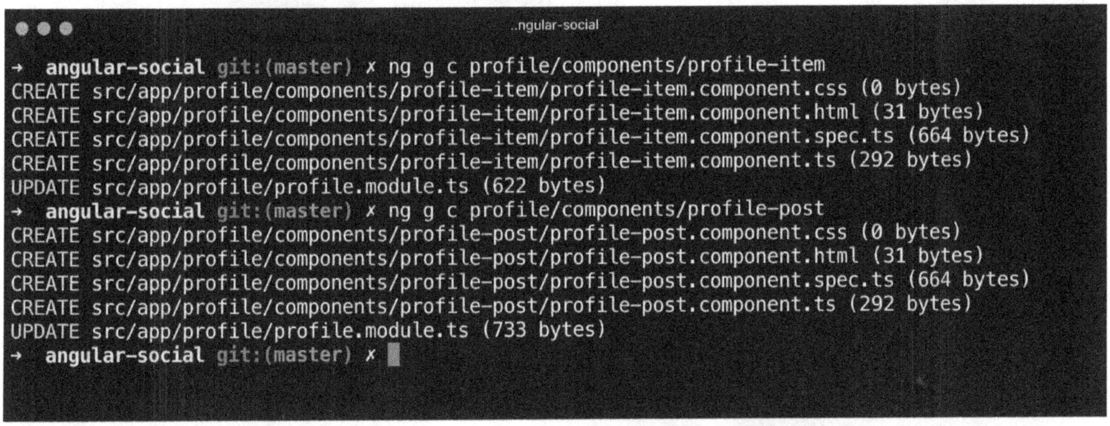

Figure 1.46: Creating the presentational components

2. Use the resolved data in the container components.

3. Create the presentational components to display the profile data from the API. The code in the **profile-item.component.html** file will look like this:

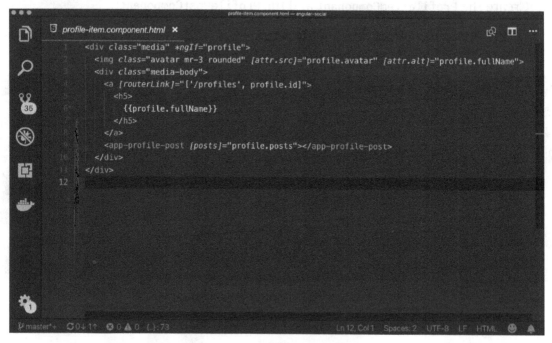

```html
<div class="media" *ngIf="profile">
    <img class="avatar mr-3 rounded" [attr.src]="profile.avatar" [attr.alt]="profile.fullName">
    <div class="media-body">
        <a [routerLink]="['/profiles', profile.id]">
            <h5>
                {{profile.fullName}}
            </h5>
        </a>
        <app-profile-post [posts]="profile.posts"></app-profile-post>
    </div>
</div>
```

Figure 1.47: The profile-item.component.html file

The code in the **profile-item.component.ts** file will look like this:

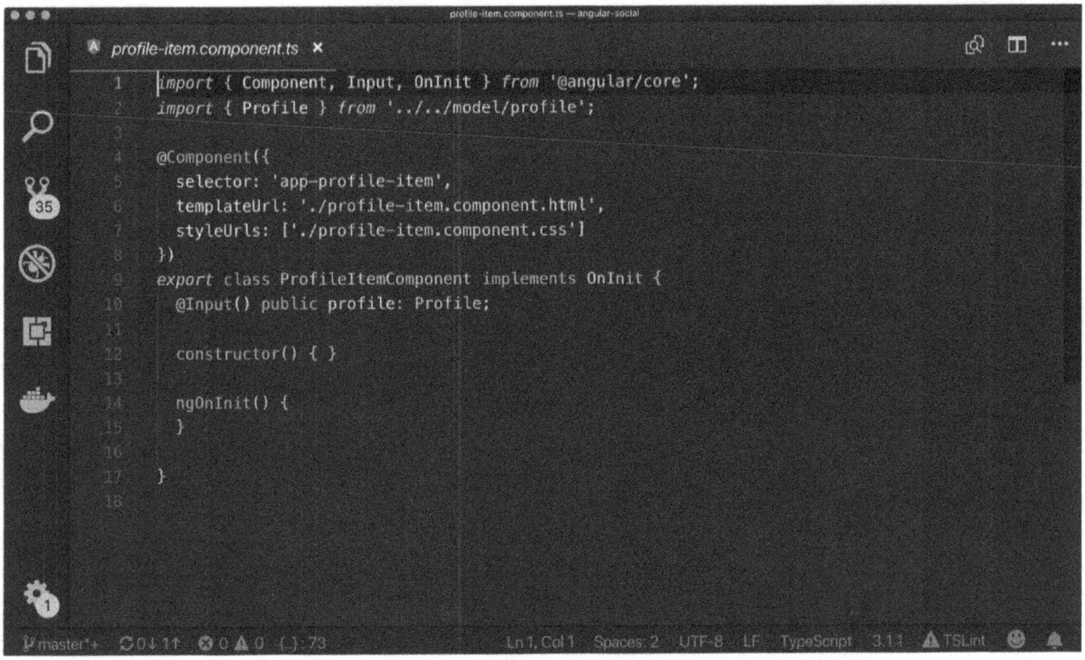
profile-item.component.ts — angular-social
profile-item.component.ts
import { Component, Input, OnInit } from '@angular/core';
import { Profile } from '../../model/profile';
@Component({
selector: 'app-profile-item',
templateUrl: './profile-item.component.html',
styleUrls: ['./profile-item.component.css']
})
export class ProfileItemComponent implements OnInit {
@Input() public profile: Profile;
constructor() { }
ngOnInit() {
}
}
Ln 1, Col 1 Spaces: 2 UTF-8 LF TypeScript 3.1.1 TSLint

Figure 1.48: The profile-item.component.ts file

The code in the **profile-post.component.html** file will look like this:

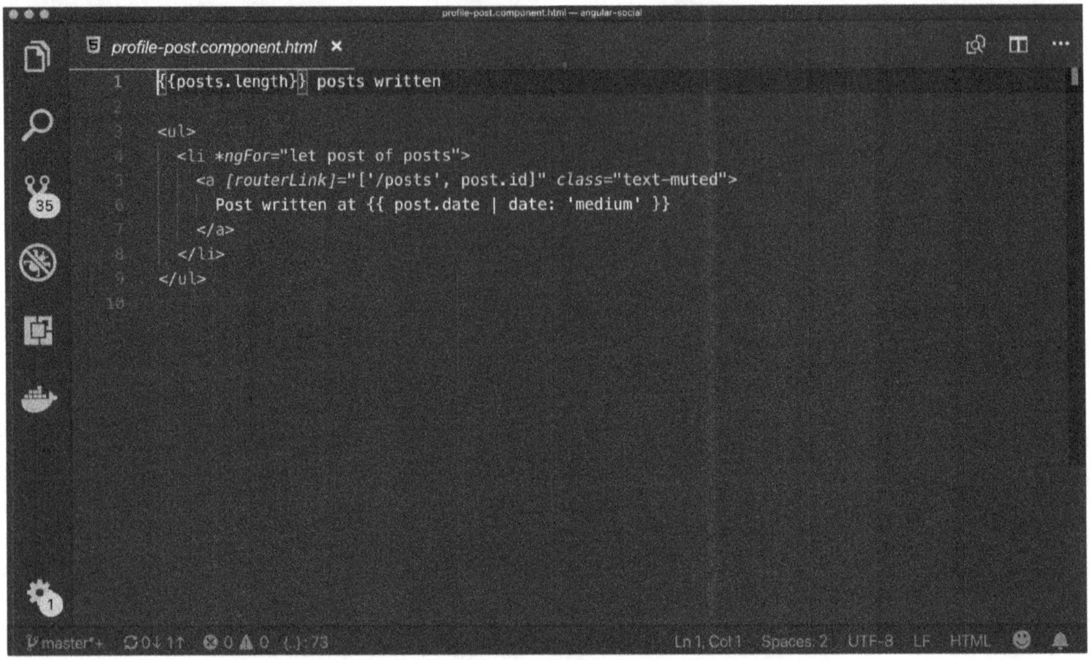

```
1   {{posts.length}} posts written
2
3   <ul>
4     <li *ngFor="let post of posts">
5       <a [routerLink]="['/posts', post.id]" class="text-muted">
6         Post written at {{ post.date | date: 'medium' }}
7       </a>
8     </li>
9   </ul>
10
```

Figure 1.49: The profile-post.component.html file

Chapter 2: Server-Side Rendering

Activity 9: Implementing the Transfer State Cache

Solution:

1. Import **TransferHttpCacheModule** from **@nguniversal/common** in **AppModule**:

   ```
   import { TransferHttpCacheModule } from '@nguniversal/common';
   ```

2. Next, import **ServerTransferStateModule** from **@angular/platform-server** in **AppServerModule**:

   ```
   import { ServerTransferStateModule } from '@angular/platform-server';
   ```

Now when you create a new build of the app, you will only see that the API request gets made once.

If you view the source of the server-side rendered page, you should see the application state as a snippet of JSON at the bottom of the page:

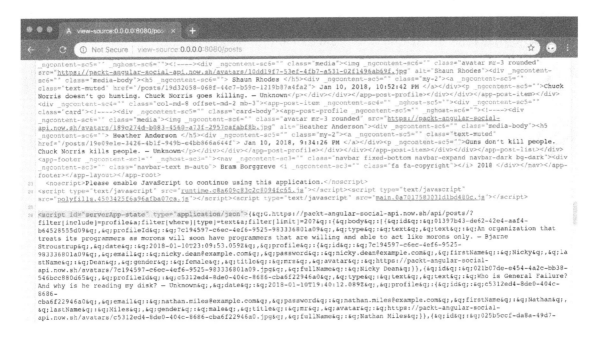

Figure 2.22: Viewing the source of the server-side rendered page

Chapter 3: Service Workers

Activity 10: Communicating with the Service Worker

Solution:

1. Open the **src/app/app.module.ts** file in your editor.

2. Import **SwPush** and **SwUpdate** from **@angular/service-worker**:

   ```
   import { SwPush, SwUpdate } from '@angular/service-worker';
   ```

3. Add a constructor and inject **SwPush** and **SwUpdate**:

   ```
   constructor(public push: SwPush, private updates: SwUpdate) {
   }
   ```

4. Add the following lines in the constructor method:

   ```
   console.log('Push enabled: ', push.isEnabled);
   console.log('Updated enabled: ', updates.isEnabled);
   ```

Now when you create a new build of the app, you will see a message being printed in the console that tells the status of the **SwPush** and **SwUpdate** classes:

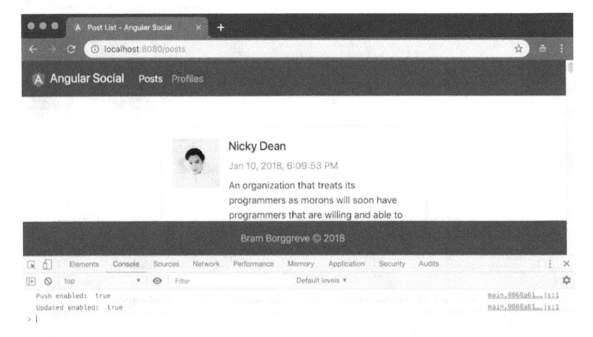

Figure 3.10: SwPush and SwUpdate messages in the console

Index

About

All major keywords used in this book are captured alphabetically in this section. Each one is accompanied by the page number of where they appear.

www.ingramcontent.com/pod-product-compliance
Lightning Source LLC
Chambersburg PA
CBHW080536060326
40690CB00022B/5148